GHOSTS
of SOMERSET

Peter Underwood
President of the Ghost Club

Bossiney Books

*First published in 1985
by Bossiney Books,
St Teath, Bodmin, Cornwall*
*Typeset and printed in Great Britain by
Blackfords of Truro
Bound by R. Booth, Bookbinders,
Mabe, Cornwall*

FOR

SHEILA and PHIL MERRITT
of Venice, California

who have already discovered
some of the joys of Somerset

ISBN 0 948158 00 X

PLATE ACKNOWLEDGEMENTS

Front cover by Mark Bygrave: King John's
Hunting Lodge, Axbridge, and the phantom cat
Back cover by Julia Davey: Site of Walford's Gibbet
All other photographs by Julia Davey
Drawings by Paul Honeywill

About the Author

Peter Underwood has been President of the Ghost Club (founded 1862) since 1960 and has probably heard more first-hand ghost stories than any man alive. A long-standing member of The Society for Psychical Research, Vice-President of the Unitarian Society for Psychical Studies, a member of The Folklore Society, The Dracula Society and a former member of the Research Committee of the Psychic Research Organization, he has lectured, written and broadcast extensively. He took part in the first official investigation into a haunting; has sat with physical and mental mediums and conducted investigations at seances, been present at exorcisms, experiments at dowsing, precognition, clairvoyance, hypnotism, regression; conducted world-wide tests in telepathy and extra-sensory perception, and has personally investigated scores of haunted houses.

He possesses comprehensive files of alleged hauntings in every county of the British Isles and many foreign countries, and his knowledge and experience has resulted in his being consulted on psychic and occult matters by the BBC and ITV.

Born at Letchworth Garden City in Hertfordshire, he now lives in a small village in Hampshire. He is Hon. Librarian of The Savage Club, 9 Fitzmaurice Place, Berkeley Square, London W1 where he can be contacted.

In 1982, Peter Underwood made his debut for Bossiney with *Ghosts of Devon*. An immediate bestseller for the cottage publishers, it was featured on BBC television from Plymouth and discussed on DevonAir.

Then in 1983, he produced *Ghosts of Cornwall* which was the subject of a Radio Cornwall series and was no. 1 bestseller in Cornwall for several months.

By the same author

Ghosts of Devon (Bossiney Books)
Ghosts of Cornwall (Bossiney Books)
This Haunted Isle (Harrap)
Ghosts of Kent (Meresborough Books)
Ghosts of Hampshire and the Isle of Wight (St Michael's Abbey Pɩ ss)
Ghosts of Wales (Christopher Davies and Corgi)
Ghosts of North-West England (Collins/Fontana)
A Ghost Hunter's Handbook (Hutchinson/Sparrow)
The Ghosts of Borley (with Dr Paul Tabori) (David & Charles)
Haunted London (Harrap and Fontana)
Hauntings – New Light on Ten Famous Cases (Dent)
A Host of Hauntings (Leslie Frewin)
A Gazetteer of British Ghosts (Souvenir Press and Pan)
A Gazetteer of Scottish and Irish Ghosts (Souvenir Press and Fontana)
Into the Occult (Harrap and Tandem)
Deeper Into the Occult (Harrap)
Lives to Remember – a Casebook on Reincarnation (with Leonard Wilder)
(Robert Hale)
The Complete Book of Dowsing and Divining (Hutchinson)
Dictionary of the Supernatural (Harrap and Fontana)
The Vampire's Bedside Companion (Leslie Frewin and Coronet)
The Ghost Hunters (Robert Hale)

AUTOBIOGRAPHY
No Common Task – the Autobiography of a Ghost Hunter (Harrap)

BIOGRAPHY
Horror Man – The Life of Boris Karloff (Leslie Frewin)
Life's a Drag – Life of Danny La Rue (Leslie Frewin)

AS EDITOR
Thirteen Famous Ghost Stories (Dent's Everyman's Library)

**Right: The Author, Peter Underwood, President
of the Ghost Club.**

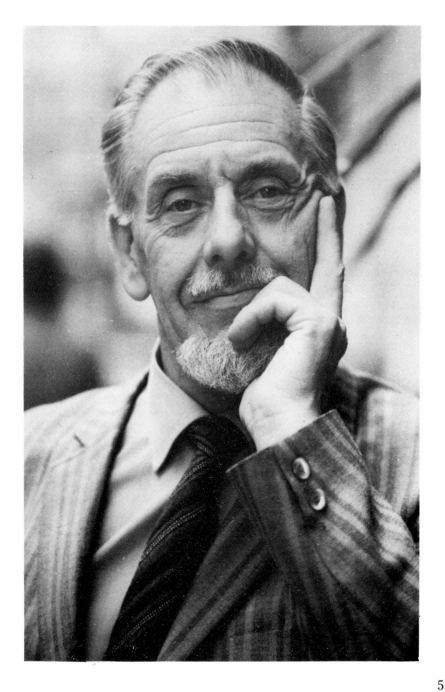

Introduction

Somerset has been called the Crescent County of the West and throughout its million acres are scores of romantic and historic houses, towns, villages and landscapes; many of them have individual ghostly associations, many are reputed to be haunted by singular paranormal activity and not a few have been the scene of repeated spectral appearances that totally defy rational explanation. Somerset is indeed a rich hunting ground for the ghost enthusiast.

Right: St Mary's Church at Yatton where walks a 'grey ghostly figure'.
Below: The cat at St Nicholas's Church, Brockley Combe, where walks the 'little lady in brown'.

In this volume I have attempted to look at a variety of well-attested and some interesting but less well-attested incidents of ghostly encounters that together make up the rich tapestry of the ghosts of Somerset and in having to be selective I have chosen to omit such well-known cases as the Sampford Peverell ghost, Mrs Leaky of Minehead, many of the strange tales about Glastonbury Abbey and Cadbury Camp with its May Day and Midsummer rituals which have all been extensively written-up in the past. I hope that what I have to say about previously published cases of haunting contain something new and perhaps throw some fresh light on these dark places.

I am, as always, deeply grateful to my wife for all her encouragement, help and company in visiting the haunted places of Somerset and to the residents of this lovely part of the world who have all welcomed us and helped me enormously; and if I have strayed a little outside the present-day limits of the county I hope I may be forgiven.

At all events I shall long remember researching material for this volume and I have hopes of carrying out some interesting investigations at some of these haunted houses in the not too distant future ...

Peter Underwood

The Savage Club
Fitzmaurice Place
Berkeley Square
London W.1.

**Right: 'After the attack the brave old woman ...
expired from fright.'**

Ghosts of Somerset

Axbridge

A corner of old England, nestling beneath the towering ridge of the Mendip Hills, visitors to Axbridge gaze at the ancient stocks, the money-changer's table of 1627, and the post where the bull was tethered when people from far and wide filled the square to see the cruel bull-baiting. And in the corner of the square there is the early Tudor merchant's house that has, it seems, a ghostly lady and a phantom cat.

King John's Hunting Lodge is now a museum of local history and archaeology and in the museum diary for a day in August 1978 there is an entry that refers to the sighting of a beautiful Elizabethan lady dressed in white, apparently sitting in the Mayoral Chair. I am told that as far as can be established this Mayoral Chair, dating from the Stuart period, came from the Guild Hall, which is now the Lamb's Hotel and a food store; it was moved to the Town Hall and then took its place in King John's Hunting Lodge when that building became a museum. One wonders whether the Elizabethan lady came with it – although associated with an earlier period – or whether she simply finds it a comfortable addition to her surroundings.

Mrs Frances Neale of the Museum Management Committee tells me she is somewhat sceptical of the ghostly Elizabethan lady and she feels that subsequent alleged sightings of this ghost have their origin in one somewhat unreliable sighting; but she is less sceptical about the phantom cat. She feels this feline phantom carries more conviction by its sheer inconsequential nature, coupled with the fact that it has been witnessed on several occasions by different hard-headed and disbelieving archaeologists! And it has only been seen during the evening hours.

Right: King John's Hunting Lodge at Axbridge.

King John's Hunting
Lodge haunted by a
ghostly lady and a
phantom cat.

A member of the Society tells me that the ghostly tabby cat has
been sighted on several occasions near the doorway to the panelled
room on the first floor, just near the top of the stairs. He is among the
five or six people who have caught a brief glimpse of the cat. The
Social Secretary once saw its tail projecting above some cardboard
storage boxes just inside the panelled room and from time to time a
member will mention that they thought they saw a cat come into the
room. Always when a thorough search is made nothing is found.

Bath

Beautiful Bath has more than its fair share of ghosts and this elegant
city can vie with York and Farnham as Britain's most haunted town.

Perhaps the best-known ghosts here are those associated with the
Garrick's Head Hotel and the Theatre Royal. There would seem to be
at least two ghosts that haunt both properties which stand together
and may once have been linked by a secret passage. Two hundred
years ago the Garrick's Head was a gaming house run by Beau Nash

and such a passage would have been a useful escape route for the young bucks of the day whenever the cards were not coming up trumps for them. Doubtless many an argument and perhaps the odd fight or duel took place hereabouts, leaving behind ghostly reminders of a past age.

A figure in Regency dress has been encountered from time to time inside the Garrick's Head Hotel; a heavily-built man wearing a long brown wig, a form that makes squeaky footsteps as it moves but leaves no footprints.

The story goes that one day, while playing cards at the gambling club, a man learned that his wife, who was present, was having a lusty affair with another of the gamblers and in his fury the jealous husband stabbed the lover to death. The man's wife, having witnessed the murder, rushed out of the room, made her way to the top of the house and there threw herself out of a window. The ghosts of both the murdered man and the unfaithful wife have been seen and sensed at the hotel.

When Peter Welch was manager of the Garrick's Head he had no doubts that ghosts walked there. 'I am well aware they revisit the

'A figure in Regency dress has been encountered inside the Garrick's Head Hotel.'

scene of their tragedy,' he said at the time. He and his wife always treated the ghosts with respect and times without number they answered a knock on the dining room door to find no-one there. 'Please come in,' they would call out. No-one ever entered and the door remained closed but there would be no more knocking that night.

Not infrequently one of the ghosts – or perhaps both of them – would move objects and once they both saw two candles rise from their holders on a sideboard without anyone touching them. They flew through the air and narrowly missed Mrs Welch's head and then fell to the floor at her feet. The female ghost is generally regarded as being responsibile for the sudden, overwhelming and quite inexplicable scent of beautiful perfume that has been experienced many times by different people in the cellar.

Earlier landlords have had similar experiences including Bill Loud who said he saw a heavy cash register lift itself from the bar and smash a chair to pieces. Another landlord Robert Simmons – and it seems that the ghosts here are most active when a new landlord takes over – reported the inexplicable movement of a bunch of keys on his first day at the hotel and subsequently he felt a distinct presence in the cellar, where a mallet disappeared for several days, and his wife reported noises on the stairs and in the attic which no-one could explain.

A number of visitors, with no knowledge of the place being haunted, have reported hearing loud thuds and bumps in the middle of the night; other visitors have heard a knock on their bedroom door and seen the handle turn but no-one is there; still others have been awakened by a ghostly laugh or found the bedroom filled with a 'strange glow'. Immediate searches have revealed no explanation for any of these happenings and next morning they learn that such disturbances are part and parcel of the haunting at the old Garrick's Head.

The Theatre Royal has a Grey Lady who sometimes sits in a box above the audience and it would appear that she is the ghost of the lady who threw herself to her death; at all events it does seem that the two ghosts overlap the two adjoining properties and treat the environment as it must once have been.

Left: The Theatre Royal has a ghost of a grey lady.

This Grey Lady has reportedly been seen just inside the theatre at a place that corresponds with where she has also been sighted on the other side of the wall in the Garrick's Head. She also haunts the corridors leading to the Lower Circle; occupying one of the stage boxes and also a box at the rear of the Lower Circle: a ghost who has appeared many times in different places to both visiting artists and attentive audiences. In 1975 most of the members of the cast of *The Dame of Sark*, starring Dame Anna Neagle, reported seeing the mysterious Grey Lady.

One of the strangest of all ghostly manifestations here or anywhere else must surely be the phantom butterfly that has appeared each Christmas at the Theatre Royal. After his father's death in 1948 Frank Maddox took over the direction of the Christmas pantomime, a feature of the production being a butterfly ballet which consisted of girls dressed as tortoiseshell butterflies; and during the first performance a 'real' tortoiseshell butterfly appeared and flew round the theatre. That was strange enough in the middle of winter but every year since then, with one single exception, the annual pantomime at the Theatre Royal has been treated to the appearance of what seems to be a tortoiseshell butterfly, but where it comes from and where it goes to nobody knows; and it always makes just the one annual appearance.

The Assembly Rooms harbour the best-documented ghost in Bath: the Man in a Black Hat; an unidentified figure whose appearance suggests he dates from the time the Assembly Rooms were built, 1771, possibly even earlier.

Margaret Royal, a city guide who is a mine of information concerning the ghosts of Bath, tells me that the evidence for this particular ghost goes back many years. There are references to the mysterious figure in eighteenth and nineteenth-century documents but sightings have continued into the present day. In 1950 Mrs Cynthia Montefiore was walking from Portland Place to George Street. Towards the end of Saville Row she saw a man approaching her. He wore a large black hat, somewhat resembling the old-fashioned Quaker headgear. He crossed the road noiselessly and came abreast of Mrs Montefiore as she reached the end of Saville Row. There was no-one else in sight and she suddenly had the

Right: The Man in the Black Hat.

feeling that there was something strange about the figure. As he passed she turned round to have another look at him and found that he had completely disappeared. There was no time for him to have entered a doorway or disappeared from view in any normal way. The moment he passed she turned round – and there was nothing to see.

Mrs Montefiore produced a sketch of the figure she had seen and this joined three other sketches made independently by three different eye-witnesses who were all strangers to each other and who had no previous knowledge of any ghostly Man in a Black Hat. All the four sketches, reproduced in Margaret Royal's book, *Local Ghosts* (1976), depict a slightly stooping figure and the predominant feature in each case is a large black hat.

In 1974 Mrs Eileen Parrish encountered the same figure. She was parking her car when she saw him come down Saville Row, step into the road, hesitate, turn back and begin to walk towards the Assembly Rooms. She took her eyes off the figure for a moment and when she looked again he had vanished. Mrs Parrish is emphatic that he could not possibly have reached the end of the road in the brief second that she was not looking at him. She said the figure was dressed much as contemporary pictures depict Guy Fawkes and, as he turned, the black cloak that he was wearing swirled around him. He wore black breeches and gaiters. It did not occur to her until after he had disappeared that she might be seeing a ghost; the figure had appeared to be perfectly normal except for his dress.

The same figure appears to have been seen in different parts of the interior of the Assembly Rooms. One witness has described watching a television film being recorded when she became aware of an oddly-dressed man standing beside her. She felt there was something vaguely unpleasant about the dark figure wearing a black hat and then suddenly the solid-looking figure she had seen was no longer standing beside her!

A former Regimental Sergeant-Major has described seeing a similar figure one morning. He became aware that someone was standing in the doorway watching him and when he turned he saw the figure of a man wearing a dark cloak and a black hat. As he stared at the strange form, which appeared to be quite solid and normal, it slowly lost substance and within seconds disappeared.

A house in Gay Street, where Dr Samuel Johnson (1709-84) was often entertained by a Mrs Thale who lived there at the time, has long been reputed to be haunted by ghost voices. The sounds of conversation have been distinctly heard on many occasions apparently emanating from the drawing room. When the door is opened the sounds cease and nothing is ever found to account for what has been heard. As with so many cases of ghost voices in haunted houses no words are distinguishable.

There is another house in the same street that was so haunted at one time that military police officers admitted to disturbances that they were unable to explain and in 1977, appropriately enough, a 'gay' male ghost, with his hair tied back with a ribbon, haunted the vicinity of Gay Street.

According to reports at the time the phantom form was seen on a number of occasions but only appeared to men; when women were present, they were unable to see the form which appeared to be solid and real to the men. One witness was the Deputy-Mayor of Miami, Scott Harris. He and his wife were taking part in a tour of Bath conducted by Margaret Royal who later told me: 'As we all walked along the path behind Gay Street, Mr Harris grew very agitated. He said the figure of a man was keeping pace with us, yet his wife and I could see nothing. Mr Harris's description of a man with white hair tied back with a ribbon matched those given by other people who say they have seen the ghost.'

When a party of thirteen-year-old schoolboys were on a tour one afternoon, one of them stood terrified at the foot of the steps leading up to the gravel path behind Gay Street. He said that a ghostly white-haired man was standing at the top of the steps. Steve Bransgrove, a resident of Bath and a student of the history of the place, was present when the same figure was seen, in daylight, and it is an experience that he will always remember. 'A middle-aged man I was talking to suddenly started babbling about a transparent white-haired man standing at the top of the steps. He was so affected by what he saw that I called for an ambulance and he was taken to hospital and treated for shock.'

A house in Pulteney Street, once the home of Admiral Howe, First Lord of the Admiralty (1783-8) and a commander of the Channel Fleet in the French War which won the 'glorious first of June' victory off Ushant in 1794, has long been reputed to be haunted. The figure of Lord Howe (1726-99) has been reported a number of times and when Mrs Sheila Haines occupied the basement flat she told Margaret Royal about the time when her husband, a policeman, had left the house at four o'clock one morning. Ten minutes later she heard footsteps outside in the passage: 'The bedroom door opened and in came this man in naval uniform. I was lying in bed. The door opened and he just walked in. He seemed to look round the room. I was speechless ... Then I heard the bedroom door shut, there were sounds of him walking back down the passage and that was it. He seemed to be quite pleasant and behaved almost as though he was checking the place. After that I saw him three more times and each time it was just as though he was an ordinary, living person.

'There was also a curious noise that seemed to accompany this manifestation. One morning in particular it sounded just as though somebody had come in soaking wet. The passageway was made of stone and as he reached the outside of my bedroom door I could visualize exactly what he was doing. I could hear him take off his hat, shake it, and then I heard him take his boots off. He seemed to have a job with his boots and I could hear him huffing and blowing. On the occasions that I heard these noises he would come into the bedroom with his boots in his hand, walk across to a recessed cupboard – and disappear.' Some years after she had left Pulteney Street, Mrs Haines had occasion to go to the house next door and the woman then living there said she had once seen a man in naval uniform come out of a wall in the house ... she had known nothing of Mrs Haines's experiences.

The house that used to belong to Frederick, Duke of York (1763-1827), named York Villa, has a ghost story dating from the boisterous days of that second son of George III who kept one of his mistresses here together with two of the couple's children.

The story goes that one day he decided to end this particular relationship and go and live in London. His mistress decided to follow him and instructed an old family retainer to look after the children while she was away herself keeping an eye on 'the grand old Duke of York' who was the subject of several scandals.

It would appear that neither the family retainer nor the other servants had been paid their wages for a long time and within weeks of the mistress of the house leaving all the servants had left too and the two young children starved to death. After a time the old retainer did return to the house and was filled with remorse when he discovered the bodies of the children whose deaths were the result of his neglect and it is said to be his ghost that has haunted York Villa ever since. In recent years the haunting takes the form of weary footsteps climbing up the stairs and then ceasing.

Pulteney Street haunted by the ghost of Admiral Howe.

The figure of the old retainer used to be seen on the same stairway and during the last war someone who was staying at the house asked the then occupant: 'Who is that person I have seen in a long cloak and dark trousers? Surely he has no right to be in the house? I met him on the stairs as I was coming down this morning ...' In fact there was no such living person in the house where fleeting glimpses of a woman in grey at the top of the building have also been reported.

The Grosvenor Hotel, once the home of poet laureate William Wordsworth (1770-1850), has a grey, misty ghost of a lady and the 'appearance' is always accompanied by a feeling of extreme coldness.

Beverly Bush, the son of the manageress, has told how early one morning he was about to enter his mother's room on the first floor when he heard footsteps that seemed to emanate from the other side of a door in the corridor. As he opened this door he encountered a grey, misty form in the shape of a woman and at the same time he experienced an icy chill; nevertheless he followed the figure when it turned right and disappeared into a large room known as the Conference Room. However, by the time he entered the room there was no sign of the figure he had seen but he noticed that a chair had been pulled back from its place at one of the long tables.

A family friend, Gordon Hall, had a similar experience here one Christmas morning. He was carrying a tray of coffee up to his flat when he heard footsteps that seemed to approach the door from the other side. He put the tray down and opened the door. He was met by an icy draught and 'a misty figure' seemed to rush past him and disappear down the corridor.

One of the helpers at the Grosvenor Hotel has related her experience when she was in the second floor corridor one morning. She saw the indistinct form of a woman leave a room, quickly cross the corridor and disappear in the direction of the stairs. Molly says the woman she saw was dressed in grey. Subsequent enquiries established that no real person was in the vicinity at the time.

Bridgwater

The area around Bridgwater is very haunted. A wood-bordered roadway that once formed part of an ancient estate has long been regarded as the haunt of a phantom black horse and also a black dog; creatures of the night that suddenly materialise and as suddenly and mysteriously disappear.

King Alfred hid hereabouts during the winter and spring of 877-8 after the Danes had overrun his kingdom and his fugitive form has been seen, hurrying for shelter, on the moorland that he knew, and the sound of primitive fighting has been heard at the places where ferocious skirmishes took place more than eleven hundred years ago.

Each 6 July, it is said, outside Bridgwater on the road to Weston Zoyland, in the sunlight of a still evening, you may hear a snatch of hymn-singing: an echo of the events of a July evening three hundred years ago when the Duke of Monmouth and his forces, retreating from Bristol to Bridgwater, engaged the royalist army and was heavily defeated; many of the battered and wounded rebels staggering through the marsh mist singing hymns to keep up their spirits ...

Another ragged and tall soldier from Sedgemoor haunts crossroads on the Bridgwater-Stogursey road, a ghost that was seen for 250 years before digging a hole for the signpost revealed the bones of a tall man. Since the ghost was always said to wear a red coat he was probably one of those who deserted to join Monmouth and was perhaps hanged at the crossroads by Colonel Kirke – and still occasionally the figure haunts the site.

In Bridgwater itself – where there is a 'Witches Walk' – there is a timber-framed seventeenth-century building in St Mary Street, called Marycourt, or more aptly perhaps, Judge Jeffreys' Lodgings, for Jeffreys stayed here and on certain unspecified nights of the year the ghostly sounds of the judge's footsteps echo down the passages and his hand knocks on the doors – notwithstanding the fact that the property now houses business premises.

Some historians maintain that Monmouth lodged in Bridgwater Castle and the ghost of the handsome, vain and dissolute favourite of Charles II is said to haunt the ruins, especially during the early days of each July. Tradition has it, however, that he spent the night before the battle of Sedgemoor at Sydenham Manor and here, too, his ghost has been known to walk; the manor is now a clubhouse that belongs to British Cellophane.

The Monmouth Room here, which contains his portrait, faces east and when he occupied it the view encompassed the open space that then was Sedgemoor. Off the bedroom there is now a bathroom, once a small closet used by Monmouth for prayers and worship. His shadowy presence haunted this bedroom and the little closet when Sydenham Manor was a private house, says Berta Lawrence; and perhaps it still does for there is a strange atmosphere here that has been remarked upon by many people.

Years ago there was a persistent story concerning a certain house in Bridgwater. It was said that late at night three taps would be heard at one of the windows, followed by the sound of something snapping. At least one witness said he not only heard these sounds but also saw the ghostly form of a man with a bag or basket – but who he was or what he wanted no-one seems to know.

Another house in the town was, and perhaps still is, haunted by the sound of ghostly footsteps, around eleven o'clock each night, followed by the sounds of a man's voice near a bedroom door. One story tells of two nieces coming to stay in the house for three weeks and their uncle who lived there told them that the room was haunted and they 'screamed with joy' and begged to be allowed to sleep in the haunted room. They slept there for a fortnight and heard the ghostly sounds almost every night. Once one of them whispered, 'Let's go and tell Aunty' but the other told her to lie still as she was afraid if she moved something might catch hold of her! They managed to make contact with the ghost, so runs the story, who told them where some gold was hidden and afterwards the ghost did not appear again while the girls were at the house.

Bristol

The ghostly figure of a black-robed monk has been reported from the vicinity of All Saints' Church, on the corner of Corn Street and High Street, for many years now and I recall Eliott O'Donnell telling me the story of hidden treasure watched over by a ghost monk ...

When Henry VIII's men were collecting all the valuable church plate they could lay their hands on, the treasured silver of All Saints', said to have been one of the treasure houses of the Westcountry, was hurriedly secreted in some part of the building, either above or below ground, and only a single priest knew the hiding-place. Here too, founded and maintained by the Guild of Calenderies, there was a famous collection of books that became the first free library in England, and a Black Monk is thought to have been a member of the Guild.

After Henry's men had carried away sacks of gold and silver and jewellery, they were still convinced that there was much more treasure somewhere on the premises and they suspected that one of the monks who had disappeared might well be responsible for hiding the treasure. They returned and ransacked the building, tearing up floorboards, breaking down walls, smashing pillars and destroying ancient carvings and woodwork and pictures but they found no treasure. Soon the Guild of Calenderies was dispersed by order of the King and then reports began to circulate concerning a ghostly Black Monk being seen in the church; usually the form was said to glide along the chancel and disappear into a stone wall.

The same figure was seen by many successive vicars and was also reported in the parsonage house, built into the south-west corner of the church. In 1830 the then vicar said he and one of his servants had seen the Black Monk and it seemed to beckon to them before disappearing into a bricked-up doorway.

In 1846 various ghostly happenings, both auditory and visual,

Right: A misty quayside in Bristol.

The Llandoger Trow:
'... haunted by the ghost of
a young crippled boy ...'

were said to occur in the vicarage. Heavy footsteps walked about the house in the middle of the night, a ghostly light flickered on one wall, doors opened mysteriously and the figure of a black-clad monk with whiskers was reportedly seen in both the house and the adjoining church.

In 1942 a fire-watcher in the vestry saw a monk-like figure standing near a wall during an air-raid; and towards Christmas 1948, a church worker, decorating a Christmas tree, saw a Black Monk walk down the aisle.

About the same period a workman came across a hitherto undiscovered trap-door in one of the aisles and a church official hurriedly summoned the vicar. With some difficulty the square door was opened to reveal a vault but it was devoid of any treasure.

A house built on the supposed site of the old churchyard of St Philip's was the scene of unexplained happenings many years ago and I recall hearing at the time about the nightly tramp of heavy footsteps up and down the stairs of the house, traversing a passage and crossing the floor of one room. The property continued to be haunted until it was eventually demolished.

The Llandoger Trow, in King Street, is one of Bristol's best-known inns. It was built in 1664 and the timbered, gable-fronted 'Trow' was known to Robert Louis Stevenson (1850-94) who described it in *Treasure Island*. Interestingly enough, according to a scroll preserved at the inn, the place takes its name from a fishing village on the River Wye and has long been associated with a Captain Hawkins who traded the Welsh Back in his trow or flat-bottomed sailing barge and, on retirement, ran the inn. It was here too that Alexander Selkirk – the real Robinson Crusoe – met Daniel Defoe and gave the world another classic story.

The inn is said to be haunted by the ghost of a young crippled boy who lived and died in the building and, although it now seems impossible to find any person living who claims to have seen the ghost, various odd happenings over the years have been attributed to it. Noises, for which no natural explanation have ever been discovered, have been heard in the area of the Old Bar and in the yard late at night when the building is otherwise quiet but when an 'uneasy silence and an eerie atmosphere' sometimes pervades the place. The ghost of the crippled boy is reputed to have been seen in the yard where one of his duties would have been to fetch water from the pump.

In the 1930s Mr and Mrs Baker lodged next door to the inn, occupying rooms that are now part of the hostelry, and they said they both heard and saw the ghost boy several times. More recently visitors have heard a noise that they have likened to footsteps but with 'an odd gait'.

The oldest theatre in Britain, the Theatre Royal, where actress Sarah Siddons (1755-1831) began her acting career, was haunted by the ghost of the finest tragedienne of the British stage before the theatre was modernised. The area of the old dressing rooms was where her ghost walked, a gentle shade returning to the theatre that she loved; but sadly she has not been seen for more than ten years now. However the actress Chili Bouchier has told me about a ghostly experience she once had at the Theatre Royal.

During one change that she had as Becky Sharpe in Thackeray's *Vanity Fair*, she found her dressing room in darkness, the carefully arranged clothing and jewellery disarranged. Suddenly the corridor

27

**Left: Bristol Gorge.
Right: Leigh Woods where
frightful screams have
been heard.**

light dimmed mysteriously and as the atmosphere became gloomy and icy cold, Chili heard the sound of light sobbing and groaning coming from a corner of the room. Subsequently she discovered that her dresser had also heard the moaning voice and had seen the light inexplicably dim on several occasions. After that the room was no longer used as a dressing room.

Leigh Woods, opposite Clifton Down, is a delightful place on a summer day but after dark, especially on winter nights, frightful screams have been heard, weird noises that have never been explained: and it is an odd fact that occasionally usually quiet dogs suddenly show all the signs of extreme terror and it may be that they see or sense something invisible to their human companions.

The famous suspension bridge here was designed by Isambard Kingdom Brunel (1806-59) but he died before it was opened. Is his the ghostly form that has repeatedly been reported here? A slightly stooping figure, hurrying along in a high-collared cut-away overcoat, a high top hat and the inevitable cigar?

28

A house in St James's Parade, off the Horsefair, has or had a ghostly disembodied face, seemingly that of an evil woman; and the reported disturbances eventually reached such a pitch that the occupants were re-housed.

Mrs H. Britton occupied a flat in the house together with her husband and three children, two grown-up and one still a baby. At first the family only complained of padding footsteps and odd tapping sounds. Several psychic investigators visited the house, sometimes spending the whole night there while Mrs Britton was in her bedroom accompanied by Mrs Gilbert, who occupied another flat in the house. Once, after a long wait, the investigators heard the mysterious tapping sounds and then, suddenly, everyone was startled by a loud scream from the direction of Mrs Britton's bedroom and on immediate investigation Mrs Britton was found lying on the floor in a faint. When she recovered she said that after the tapping sounds had begun the atmosphere in the bedroom had seemed to change; it had become 'cold and horrible' and the walls had seemed to quiver. She had looked towards the door and had seen the horrible face of a woman moving towards her sleeping baby. She had hurled herself at the form and that was all she remembered. On this occasion Mrs Britton was alone in her bedroom apart from the baby.

A few days later the Brittons' flat was wired-up to record any sound and at 2.15 a.m. Mrs Britton had exactly the same experience and again she collapsed in a faint. This time she had a companion with her but Mrs Gilbert saw nothing although she confirmed that suddenly Mrs Britton had stood up, put out her hands, went completely stiff, cried out and had then fallen face-forward to the floor. Afterwards Mrs Britton said she had again seen the 'horrible face of an old woman' moving towards the baby's cot and she had attempted to get between the form and the cot. The next thing she knew was when she found herself recovering consciousness on the floor.

It was after the appropriate medical officer of health had heard the recording that had been obtained in the house and had received a full report from the investigators, that the family was re-housed. Subsequently the property became a business premises. It is reported to stand on the site of a Benedictine priory.

Seventeenth-century Oldbury House on St Michael's Hill was badly haunted when it was occupied by a number of girls during the 1940s. The BBC took over the house as a hostel and for a time the twenty-eight girls residing there were looked after by Miss G.M. Brownlee, a Westcountry photographer who was bombed out of her London home. She slept on the ground floor and soon found her nights disturbed by thuds, dragging noises and the sound of a child sobbing. And then she saw the ghosts.

First there was a very tall, thin man, dressed like a monk in a long, dark robe, with a bunch of keys hanging from a girdle at his waist; next there was a little old woman, dressed like an old-fashioned housekeeper; and finally there were five ladies who were always seen together, dressed alike in clinging robes with high head-dresses. The five women seemed to be talking agitatedly among themselves and sometimes Miss Brownlee saw the five ladies with

Right: '... a phantom form was encountered ... a cowled figure wearing a sort of cloak.'

30

the ghost monk in the background, looking as though he was pleading for something.

Miss Brownlee said nothing of what she heard and saw to the girls but before long eight of them told her of 'presences' they had seen in the hostel. After only three months the repeated ghost sightings began to affect all the occupants and the hostel was closed.

True ghost stories often turn up in the most unexpected places and a correspondent has sent me a cutting from a 1978 issue of *Insurance Monitor* where an interesting ghost sighting is recounted in the vicinity of Phoenix House on Redcliff Hill.

David Hine, a London area manager, recalled that a colleague from Bristol told him of the reluctance of some of the staff to remain after hours at the very modern building in Redcliff Hill, because it was reputed to be haunted.

He thought little about the matter until he remembered his own time in Bristol, at the old Phoenix office in Clare Street, from 1957 to 1964. At that time he and other members of the staff would often pop out for a quick coffee and he recalled Redcliff Hill as it used to be, very narrow and crowded with old houses and shops. He and his associates at the time would frequently see a lady, who seemed to be far from well, talking endlessly to herself, and invariably she would be weighed down and slung about with cases and carrier bags which seemed to contain clothing and all sorts of possessions. Time after time they saw her muttering her way through the street.

In 1978, on a social occasion, David Hine found himself sitting next to a data processing manager from Bristol who told him that several of his staff claimed to have seen an apparition. Without revealing anything of his own experiences David Hine asked about the appearance of the so-called ghost and learned that it was 'an old lady carrying lots of things'. On a later visit to Bristol he made a number of enquiries and was told that the old lady was a well-known local character; she had been bombed out during the war and had lost all her possessions and some of her mental faculties. In fear of a repetition of the terrible experiences from that time onwards she carried all that she possessed wherever she went.

Vassall Park, Fishponds, is reputedly haunted by the ghost of a former Duchess of Beaufort and many people over the years have claimed to see her ghostly figure usually riding through the park as she did so many times during her lifetime. Quite recently a different phantom form was encountered by two teenagers halfway across the footbridge that spans the River Frome, a cowled figure wearing a sort of cloak; as the youngsters approached the figure turned back and vanished, seemingly into a wall near the end of the bridge.

At the spot where the figure vanished other witnesses have reported seeing a ghost monk; others again have heard monks chanting and still others have reported seeing an inexplicable white light floating close to the wall. According to old Lady Vassall a monk was bricked-up alive inside this wall many years ago for some forgotten sin.

Brockley

Brockley Court, Brockley Combe, a fourteenth-century manor house with a ghost that had, apparently, been photographed, first came to my attention nearly forty years ago. Subsequently I discussed the case at some length with Elliott O'Donnell who always regarded the picturesque Elizabethan property as 'badly haunted'. 'There are at least six ghosts in the area,' he told me, 'and I'm certain I saw one at Brockley Court.'

I asked him about the six ghosts; were they really different ghosts or manifestations of the same haunting entity, I wondered. 'Oh quite different, I assure you,' he replied and proceeded to list the ghosts long associated with Brockley Combe.

Briefly they were differentiated as the Ghostly Horseman, said to ride down the Combe around midnight on moonlit nights; the Bounding Ghost, a tall, thin form of indefinite sex who bounded noiselessly along the road ahead of travellers and disappeared, disconcertingly, among some trees; the Phantom Girl, the ghost of a young woman who died of a broken heart after a tragic love affair; the ghostly Dinah Swan, a ninety-year-old woman – maybe the same ghost we meet at Wookey Hole – who was found dead in her cottage, 'supposed to have been frightened to death' according to the inquest 'by some person or persons unknown'; the Phantom Coach which is supposed to race through Brockley Combe, driven by a man dressed in nineteenth-century clothes, cracking his whip in the air, although making no sound, until the whole thing vanishes into thin air; and finally the Ghost Man, a form that was always seen standing beneath a tree in a triangle of grass half way up the Combe.

The area is also said to be haunted by the ghost of a parson named

Hibbetson, a wicked man who rescued the Squire of Chelvey one day when he was injured, nursed him back to health and then, having made sure that the Squire's will had been altered in his favour, lost no time in murdering him!

Details of most of the alleged ghosts at Brockley are thin on the ground although the ghost of Dinah Swan seems to be fairly well established. Her cottage was broken into with some violence, the lock and bolt of the door being torn from their fastenings and a number of valuables were taken. After the attack the brave old woman seems to have dragged herself as far as the heavy iron gates of a nearby big house and there expired from fright. Her ghost was only seen after midnight when, presumably, the dastardly event originally took place. During the last war a lady from Weston-super-Mare reported seeing the figure of an old woman in great distress in the vicinity, a figure that disappeared when she approached, and such details as were supplied suggested that it was the ghost of old Dinah Swan who died very early one December morning in 1833.

The Ghost Man has also been reported several times at the same spot by different people who have been unaware of previous sightings. One described the figure as 'dressed in black with a white blob in the front that looked like a large white collar'; most witnesses said the figure 'seemed to stand out from its surroundings' and one moment it was there, as clear and distinct as could be, and the next moment it was gone.

Brockley Court or Manor was certainly long regarded as haunted and at one period it stood empty for some eighteen years because of its haunted reputation, it is said. For more than sixty years periodical reports were published concerning the house and its ghost and when Elliott O'Donnell heard about some of the sightings he made enquiries and subsequently visited the house several times. A ghost hunter of repute he visited haunted houses in the company of Lord Curzon, Sir C. Aubrey Smith, Sir Arthur Conan Doyle and the then Duke of Newcastle.

O'Donnell first visited Brockley Court, reputed to have been the house 'in which and around which' Wilkie Collins wrote his atmospheric story *The Woman in White* (first published in 1860), in the company of a journalist from Bristol, where O'Donnell lived for many years. At two o'clock in the morning a dog they had taken with them suddenly showed signs of extreme fear, whining and snarling for no apparent reason. Shortly afterwards both watchers saw a curious pillar of light move across the room and vanish close to a window. O'Donnell always believed this manifestation to be superphysical in origin and at the time he addressed whatever entity might be present, requesting a further appearance of some kind. But he received no reply or response to his request and when nothing further happened, he and his companion left the house an hour or so later.

O'Donnell visited the house a second time accompanied by three friends and this time they meticulously examined the house from top to bottom and then settled themselves in what had become known as 'the haunted room', situated off a corridor that led to the main staircase.

They had expected another friend to join them but hour after hour passed uneventfully until, close to one o'clock in the morning, they heard the front door bell ring. In a body they went down to investigate and discovered their erstwhile companion had walked some eight miles to join them! Having learned that nothing had

A ghost has been photographed at Brockley Court.

happened in the 'haunted room' he suggested that the party split up and endeavour to keep watch in several parts of the house but O'Donnell and his companions were convinced that if anything was going to happen it would happen in the room they were occupying so it was arranged that they would continue their vigil in the 'haunted room' and the new arrival positioned himself at the end of the corridor outside that room, near the top of the stairs, as a look-out.

All was quiet for a further two hours and then the three watchers were startled to hear calls for help. On running to see what had happened they found their companion in considerable distress. He told them he had fallen asleep and in a dream or on waking, he was not sure which, he had seen a tall man with a dreadful face come leaping up the stairs, bound past him and enter the room where his companions were keeping watch. The description that he gave of the figure, such as it was, interested O'Donnell for it seemed to resemble the description of one of the ghosts that were said to haunt the house, a description given to him by the owner of the property and not known to the startled watcher in the corridor.

At length all four ghost hunters returned to the 'haunted room' and resumed their long wait but nothing further happened for an hour or so and then at about four o'clock in the morning, one of the party sat up and said: 'Look here, I've had enough. I'm going home.' He had no sooner uttered these words than he added in a distraught voice, 'Oh, my God, there it is ...!' and he fell back in his chair in terror.

The others looked round the room but could see nothing and when they asked their companion what he had seen, he was too distressed to answer coherently. Suddenly O'Donnell noticed a red rectangular light some six or seven feet from the ground for which they could find no rational explanation and which had certainly not been there previously. Wondering whether this was some sort of superphysical manifestation O'Donnell quietly asked whether there was anything they could do to help and before he could say any more, one of his companions called out: 'It's going towards you!' and for a moment, O'Donnell told me, he felt distinctly uncomfortable. Afterwards, huddled around a light, his friends told him that,

Left: Brockley Combe has six ghosts in the area .

directly after they had called out, the thing, whatever it was, had apparently passed clean through Elliott O'Donnell!

By this time the watcher who had experienced something in the corridor had somewhat recovered his composure and he said that what he had seen had been a very tall figure, a man with a long, swarthy, skull-like face that was 'indescribably horrible'. For a while a light was kept on in the 'haunted room' and then the watchers resumed their vigil in darkness. Soon the man who was convinced that he had seen something suddenly called out: 'There it is again!' in a tone so full of terror and fright that O'Donnell was concerned and he hurriedly switched on the light. No-one else had seen anything and O'Donnell decided that it would be best to bring the visit to an end. They left the house convinced that a ghost of sorts, 'possibly of the elemental order', had appeared in their midst and that they had seen it in various stages of development.

Later O'Donnell returned to the house yet again, this time accompanied by Lord Curzon and a professional photographer and although they sat up for two consecutive nights in the 'haunted room', nothing happened. Subsequently O'Donnell visited the house yet again, this time with two companions, one an old school friend and the other a war correspondent who armed himself with a camera – and a revolver!

Soon after two o'clock in the morning O'Donnell's two companions declared that they could both see a number of spherical lights floating across the room followed by a smoky mist. Although O'Donnell could see nothing he suggested that the war correspondent take a photograph. This he did and the result showed the face of an evil-looking monk. Several attempts were made to exorcise the ghost following O'Donnell's investigations but he told me it made no difference and the house and its grounds continued to be haunted for many years. There was some confusion over another faked photograph taken at the house by a student who, according to Mr Adrian Conan Doyle, writing in 1945, subsequently saw the real ghost and never did any more ghost faking!

In 1947 the property was occupied by Mrs Lilian Blair and her family who stated that they had not seen the hooded monk that was

Right: Brockley Court: The photograph 'showed the face of an evil-looking monk.'

**St Nicholas Church,
Brockley Combe.**

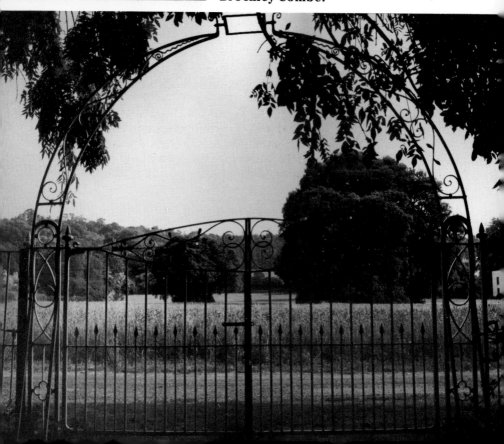

reputed to haunt the place and Mrs Blair said at the time: 'The only Supernatural thing while we have been here – only six months I might add – has been a strong smell of tobacco which we are totally unable to account for. My husband and I sleep in the room where the ghost monk is supposed to have been murdered and I was petrified one night when I heard a loud "swooshing" noise in the corridor outside, but it was only a bat!'

Some thirty years ago I was in touch with the Reverend Eric Rokeby Maddock, at that time rector at St Nicholas Church, Brockley Combe, which I had read was haunted at that time by the apparition of a 'little brown lady', mysterious footsteps, whisperings and other unexplained happenings.

Several people claimed to have seen this 'little lady in brown', either seemingly cleaning in the vestry or trotting along the aisle towards the altar. The apparition was thought to be the ghost of an elderly church worker who died in 1907. Elliott O'Donnell spent a night in the church with Everard Fielding, an investigator from the Society for Psychical Research, and a reporter. Having made a thorough examination of the church, they sealed all the doors and waited.

The watchers did not see the 'little lady in brown' but they all heard footsteps and 'strange whisperings' which they were totally unable to explain. Elliott O'Donnell told me that he understood the 'little woman in brown' had died a natural death and he thought her ghost may be drawn to the church out of sentiment. Mr Maddock said his wife was very upset about the publicity and added: 'We are without a church cleaner and it will now be more difficult than ever to get one – also to get people to attend to the altar flowers.' I heard no more about the 'little lady in brown' so I hope that she found rest and that the rector found a new church cleaner.

Cannington

Maude de Meriett lived here long ago in the days of Magna Carta and her heart is buried a few miles away at Combe Florey.

She lived at a nunnery where now a seventeenth-century house stands with earlier work incorporated in the structure. The story goes that Maude was one of three nuns who transgressed their vows and she was so severely beaten by way of punishment that she died.

And it is said to be her ghost that has been seen at the nearby Blue Anchor Inn.

When I was there I learned that the figure of a sad-faced nun had been seen walking along an upstairs corridor, crossing the little bridge over the brook that runs nearby and looking in at the windows of the inn. The wife of the licensee told me she had seen the ghost many times, adding pensively, 'But whenever I try to talk to her, she disappears.' A ghost that never seems to have frightened anyone, a quiet shade returning to the region she once knew long ago.

Chard

A town that has seen much history, today Chard slumbers after its heady historical associations. Charles I's men marched down the wide straight street that the Romans built, the street where there is a stream running down each side and dividing at the foot to go two ways: one goes south to pour itself into the English Channel while the other goes north to the Bristol Channel!

Monmouth rallied his men here and the infamous Judge Jeffreys, First Baron of Wem, held court in a building that is little changed since his day. His harsh judgments resulted in the hanging of a dozen men on a large oak tree at the end of the town; and he lodged at Chough's Hotel where his ghost is said to walk in an upstairs room and occasionally his form has been glimpsed crouching by the fireplace in the bar.

That is where he was seen by a retired policman a few years ago. It was a Sunday morning and the customer, who had been sitting in the bar, went up to the counter and asked Mrs Peters, the wife of the landlord, about the 'old man' sitting by the fire. She replied, 'There's nobody there.' 'Well, there was,' the ex-policeman replied. 'He looked a nasty old chap too, crouched over on the righthand side of the fireplace ...'

Twenty years ago a visitor recounted her experience during a night she spent at Chough's Hotel. Mrs Doreen Jones and a friend took rooms at the hotel in the middle of the town purely by chance, Mrs Jones being shown a room overlooking the main street while her friend took a room at the back of the property.

Late that night Mrs Jones heard the landlord and his wife pass her

The Blue Anchor Inn at Cannington, haunted by a nun.

bedroom on their way to bed and then all was quiet and she was soon fast asleep. Suddenly she found herself wide awake and as she lay wondering what had awakened her, she heard voices, whispering and soft laughter. After a while she got out of bed and listened at the door, then quietly opened it and peered out but there was not a soul in sight and now all was quiet.

As soon as she was back in bed the voices began again. They had a soft sound, perhaps women's voices, whispering gently and occasionally laughing. There was also a more forceful voice that occasionally intervened, a voice with 'more than a hint of malice in it ...' Again Mrs Jones got out of bed and this time she went to the window and looked out to see whether there was anyone in the street outside but it was completely deserted and there were no lights in any of the windows of nearby houses. Again she went back to bed and lay there, perfectly still, waiting; and once again she heard the light, muffled sound of female voices.

As she lay listening, puzzled as to their origin, she heard the more forceful voice seeming to gain ascendancy and again she thought she could detect a note of malice and spitefulness; she began to feel frightened and ran out of the room and took refuge with her friend at the back of the hotel.

Next morning she started to broach the subject to the landlady at breakfast but she seemed reluctant to talk and after serving the two ladies, she disappeared into the back of the hotel and did not reappear. When they were about the leave Mrs Jones seized her opportunity and asked the landlady whether there had been a party the previous night. The landlady looked at her somewhat oddly and said they were the only visitors at the hotel that night.

Some years later Mrs Jones found herself again in Chard, accompanied by her husband, and she decided to call at the Chough's to find out whether the atmosphere there still affected her. She discovered that the hotel had changed hands and over a drink she related her experience to the new landlord.

He told her that she was not the only guest to have such experiences and he said one man who had occupied the room she had slept in dashed downstairs at first light with his baggage and departed in great haste. Across his face there was a red weal such as might have been inflicted by a riding whip – a sensation he had had during his night in the room, after he had heard female voices and laughter.

44

Nor was this man the only visitor to be affected by that particular room but the landlord was not particularly keen to discuss the matter at length although he did say that some members of the Society for Psychical Research had spent an interesting night there following a number of reports the Society had received. And then he revealed that the hotel had been modernised and what had seemed to be a solid wall at the head of the bed in the 'haunted' room was found to be in fact a dividing wall hiding a small chamber which historians said had probably been a ladies' retiring room. The landlord told Mrs Jones that after the structural alterations were completed no more disturbances had been reported.

The widow of a previous landlord at Chough's, where a mummified chough or Cornish raven is preserved, has recounted coming face to face with a ghostly figure in armour at the hotel. It was about nine o'clock one evening and the landlady had gone upstairs to get some change for the bar. On her way back, outside the door of the so-called 'haunted' bedroom, she encountered a figure in armour with chains on his wrists and ankles. They were holding a carnival at Chard that night and her first thought was that one of the contestants had found his way into the private area of the hotel. He stood blocking her way and she said 'Please let me pass', whereupon the seemingly solid and real figure suddenly disappeared. It was the only experience of its kind that she ever had but understandably one she never forgot. On this landing, close to the door of Jeffreys's bedroom, with the Jeffreys coat-of-arms in plaster bas relief on the wall, a little girl is said to have been raped and murdered centuries ago.

Other alterations at Chough's have included the exposure of a fireplace and a tombstone that had been hidden behind a false wall in the bar. Whether the tombstone with its weathered marks that look like the name 'Winifred' has anything to do with the ghostly happenings is not known but many people who have tried to photograph the tombstone with a flash have either found that their apparatus will not work or the resulting photograph is fogged.

Other reported incidents at Chough's Hotel over the years include loud knockings near the back door; an unexplained figure passing a window to the yard which has been found to be deserted; the occasional movement of objects, especially in the bar, and the phantom form of a little old lady that has been seen in the corridor leading to the back door.

Chilton Cantelo: The skull of Theophilus Broome
is kept at Higher Chilton Farm.

Chilton Cantelo

A screaming skull will stand all sorts of abuse except that of moving
it from its place of rest. Past experience has convinced the owners
of the skull of Theophilus Broome – or Brome – at Higher Chilton
Farm, opposite the church, that the skull is best left in its chosen
resting place.

Broome died at the house on 18 August 1670 aged sixty-nine years
and on his deathbed he requested that his head should be preserved
in the house for evermore. The reason for this strange request is not
difficult to guess. Broome, a native of Warwickshire, had been
against the monarchy in the Civil War and he had moved to
Somerset to avoid the enmity of those he had opposed for he had no
wish to share the fate of Oliver Cromwell whose body was hanged on

the gibbet at Tyburn and his head exhibited on a spike on London Bridge.

Incidentally Cromwell's head was in the possession of Canon Wilkinson of Woodbridge, Suffolk, some years ago and when he showed it to me the hole, made when it was exhibited, was plainly visible. Much of the hair was still clinging to it and even the famous wart was still visible on the enbalmed face.

In the middle of the last century, Mrs Kerton told me years ago when she showed me the famous skull, Broome's tomb in the north transept of Chilton Cantelo church was opened and the skeleton inside was found to be headless which seems to confirm the generally accepted story. At all events burial of the head over the years, Mrs Kerton informed me, has always resulted in the manifestation of 'horrid noises'.

At first, successive tenants of the farm sought to rid themselves of the morbid relic but as soon as they began to bury the skull they were 'deterred by horrid noises portentive of sad displeasure', and the skull was returned to its resting place inside the old farmhouse.

The last attempt at burial would seem to have been in the 1860s when a sexton dug the grave himself in the churchyard with a view to giving the skull proper burial once and for all but just as he completed the digging his spade broke in two pieces and the worried sexton vowed 'never more to attempt an act so evidently repugnant to the quiet of Broome's head'.

And it does seem that it is only attempted burial that upsets the head for in 1826 during structural alterations at the farm, some workmen took it in turns to use the skull as a mug for their beer – without anything untoward being reported to occur.

On the other hand in 1977 some researchers examined the skull, two of them moving it with their bare hands and making jocular remarks about its potency. On the way back to London one of the men thought he saw a car coming straight towards him and he swerved and crashed; the other man dropped a match into his trouser turn-up and his leg was badly burned. Both men were convinced that their misfortunes were the result of handling Broome's skull.

The skull is usually kept in a cabinet specially made for it over a door in the hall of the farm, where it has been for over two hundred years; a silent reminder of human superstition and belief in the vanity of earthly life.

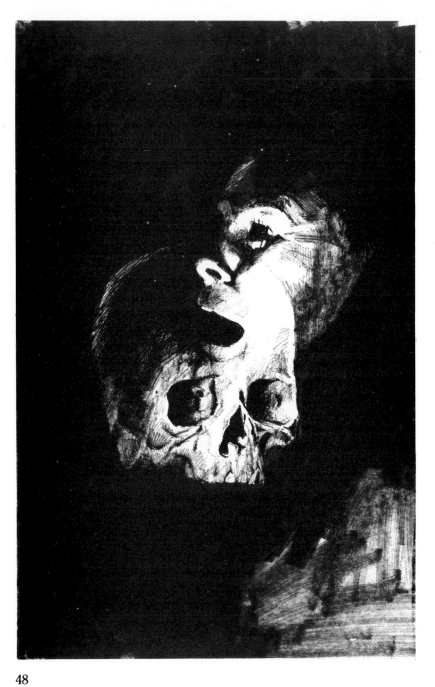

Culmhead, Blagdon near Taunton

When my wife and I stayed at the Holman Clavel Inn we both found ourselves awake in the small hours and we heard the sound of skittle balls being thrown along the skittle alley and scattering the pins. At the time we knew nothing or very little about any reputed ghost at this whitewashed, stone, six-hundred-year-old pub other than the reported sound of footsteps.

Next morning, when we commented that the skittle alley was being used very late the previous night, we learned that the sounds we had heard constituted the main haunting of the Holman Clavel, sounds that have been heard by many of the people who stay at this hostelry, once a resthouse for monks on pilgrimage to Glastonbury and later a bailiff's cottage. The skittle alley, which we saw and explored, was added much later after the property had become an inn – and it is always locked and bolted at closing time.

The ghost here is known locally as 'Charlie' and he is thought to be responsible not only for the after-hours skittle bowling but also for the footsteps in the passage leading to the bathroom. Once the son of the licensee was in the bathroom when he heard footsteps approaching the closed door and watched in wonder as the doorhandle turned and the door opened. He said afterwards that he felt an unmistakable presence as he heard the footsteps enter through the doorway, move across the room, then leave the room, close the door and pad away back along the passage. This man, a Colonial policeman home on leave, was considerably shaken by the experience.

Other disturbances at the Holman Clavel include the sound of heavy furniture being moved; occasionally too there is a noise like heavy masonry falling that has no rational explanation; and 'terrific crashing noises' like a lot of glass being broken; but nothing is ever found to account for the sounds. And from time to time small objects disappear and reappear elsewhere on the premises.

'Charlie' is reputed to be a monk who was defrocked for some

Left: 'A screaming skull will stand all sorts of abuse except that of moving it ...'

undisclosed reason. His ghostly form has occasionally been seen in one of the bedrooms, standing beside a wash basin.

Dunster

What remains of the Norman castle stands on a hill and it had a proud history. One of only a dozen Norman castles in Somerset which were dismantled or destroyed by war, it was held for the Empress Matilda against King Stephen by William de Mohun, who coined his own money here even while Stephen's forces surrounded him – and it may be from this period that the ghostly sound of clinking coins has been preserved in some way which we do not understand for such a noise has repeatedly been reported and especially on nights of the full moon.

The castle came into the possession of the King during the Civil War and then, according to Arthur Mee, after 160 days of furious fighting it passed out of royal hands but not before Blake, annoyed by the long resistance of Colonel Wyndham, threatened to put the colonel's mother in front of the fighting line, but was too proud to carry out his threat when the old lady gallantly told her son to do his duty. And it may be from this period of history that an elderly phantom form, dressed in mid-seventeenth-century costume, stalks haughtily about the old castle precincts; especially it seems when there is a thunder storm hereabouts.

The Leather Room, in the surviving castle Gateway, with its three-hundred-year-old leather hangings depicting the story of Antony and Cleopatra is, I am told, haunted from time to time by the ghostly figure of a Roundhead soldier who disappears through a closed door in the corner of the room. No sound accompanies the spectral appearance and no-one knows who the figure is or why he occasionally appears.

A correspondent tells me that she saw what she can only think must have been a ghost in The Nunnery in 1964, while staying there with her husband. They were returning from a holiday in Cornwall and stopped at The Nunnery on Sunday 27 September. Like so much

Left: The Nunnery, Dunster: '... I screamed and the shape melted away.'

of Dunster the Nunnery is very old and a beautiful building, the sort of building that my correspondent and her husband thoroughly enjoyed visiting.

Unfortunately, or perhaps fortunately, the room they occupied made my correspondent feel very uneasy as soon as she entered it. But let her tell the story in her own words: 'My husband went back to the car for our cases and immediately I felt threatened in the room in broad daylight; something I have never felt before or since. We had a meal and walked around the town before returning for the night. There were three single beds in the room but I felt so frightened that my husband and I shared one bed.

'During the night I woke suddenly and saw a figure standing at the foot of the bed. I was not aware of a face, just a white outline of a bareheaded person dressed in flowing robes. I screamed and the shape melted away quickly as if it was a light that had suddenly been turned off. My husband saw nothing and thought the whole affair very amusing indeed. The room was quite light and I was not dreaming. I was very wide awake when I saw "it".

'We never asked about it in the morning when we left, something I have regretted ever since. I found the whole affair rather embarrassing; I still do actually. People obviously think I am rather strange if I mention it and they don't believe it could possibly happen, I suppose – but it did.'

The reason that this lady wrote to me describing her experience was primarily to enquire whether I had any information regarding the possible haunting of The Nunnery and I had to say that at that time I did not seem to have any record of any other ghost sighting there, but subsequently I have had occasional reports from people having a similar experience in one of the bedrooms and on one occasion two sisters woke simultaneously to see the figure of a monk standing in the room; a figure that disappeared within seconds of the sisters waking; an experience which would be regarded by psychical researchers as a hypnagogic vision.

East Chinnock

The Chinnock triplets, East, Middle and West, lie in a straight line along the hills near Crewkerne. East Chinnock church has a font with a Norman base – and a haunted rectory.

I am indebted to Miss Cynthia Burr of New Milton for this story and I cannot do better than quote verbatim the account she was kind enough to write out for me in May 1984:

'It was an evening in early autumn – I think it must have been autumn as the oil lamps were alight and we had the oil stove burning in the playroom. This was an upstairs room at one end of the long landing, and my brother and I were playing with our model farms and soldiers on the floor. It must have been around the year 1927 as I was about five years old and my brother would have been eleven and a half.

'Suddenly I heard a bump against the outside wall by the window, and then the unmistakable sound of feet – plonk, plonk, plonk – ascending the rungs of a ladder. I glanced at my brother; he had stopped playing and had obviously heard the sounds too. We looked at each other and then he scrambled to his feet, saying "Come on!" I remember I didn't say a word but we both dashed out of the playroom, down the stairs, and into the dining room where our parents were sitting. There was one thought in our minds: a burglar was trying to get in through the playroom window. We told our parents what we had heard: the distinct sounds of a ladder being put up against the window and footsteps climbing up it.

'My father immediately rushed out into the garden and round to the side of the house where the playroom was, expecting to see the ladder and catch the intruder. But when he got there, there was no sign of a ladder and no sign of any intruder.

'My brother and I still recall those moments when, simultaneously, we both heard that ladder and those footsteps. Had only one of us heard the sounds, we would have put it down to imagination, but we both heard exactly the same sounds and we both thought of burglars. Neither of us had the slightest idea of ghosts and indeed it was not until many years later that we heard the story of the haunted rectory ...

'It was the Old Rectory, in fact the building is about 450 years old. In the beginning it had been an ordinary large house and it became the Rectory in the late eighteenth century. An extra wing was added when one of the rectors had seven daughters. Whether this story relates to the seventh daughter I'm not sure, but it may well be so.

'It seems there was a daughter of the house who was very beautiful. She had long fair hair and blue eyes, and she fell in love with a young man of whom her parents did not approve. As her

53

father would under no circumstances consent to their marriage, they made up their minds to elope. So one night, when it was dark, the young man procured a ladder, climbed up to the girl's room and brought her safely down. Presumably they were then driven off in a waiting coach-and-horses, for it is said, if one is very lucky, the sound of galloping horses may be heard going down the village street at midnight! I never heard those horses, nor did I ever come across anyone who had heard them, but for miles around the story of the haunted rectory was well known, and when my father first went there, six years before I was born, the neighbouring clergy and their wives remarked to my mother about her living in a haunted house.

'Another, much less pleasant, version of the story is that the young couple did not elope but the girl told the young man she did not wish to marry him. Then, it was said, the distraught young man got a ladder, climbed through the window into the girl's bedroom and murdered her. I do not like this version of the story but it would account for the distinct feeling of unease which I always felt in the house when I was a child, even though I was born there and spent the first seventeen years of my life there.

'My father, who was a very sensible man, seems to have actually seen the ghost. He awakened my mother one night to tell her that a young girl with long fair hair was standing in front of the dressing-table mirror over by the window. By the time my mother was fully awake, the vision had vanished. Another time my father apparently saw the same girl walking across the lawn in the garden; and once again she simply vanished as he watched.

'Recently, when discussing the ghost story with my older cousin – she is the daughter of my mother's sister who died in 1958 – she told me that my mother said I had seen the ghost when I was only two or three years old. Apparently I told her that a beautiful lady with pretty long hair had stood by my bed and looked at me in the night! But I do not remember seeing her. However the description certainly resembled those given by my father; and my bedroom was a small dressing-room leading out of my parents' bedroom.

'Two years ago my brother and I called at the Old Rectory. It is no longer a rectory and the lady whose husband had bought it welcomed us warmly and was most interested to learn that we once lived there. She, too, had heard the ghost story – the elopement version – and, being interested in psychical research, she was delighted to be living in a reportedly haunted house. She said she had the feeling it had been a very happy house but she also had seen a ghost; a different one. This was a white-haired old clergyman, dressed in the old-fashioned clerical grey worn in olden days, who appeared to her late one night in the kitchen. He was smiling and looked very happy. She saw him for a minute or two, and then he vanished.

'My parents lived in the rectory for twenty-four years. During that time it would seem that my father saw the ghost twice while my mother never saw or heard anything. My brother and I heard the ghostly sounds once; neither of us saw anything; unless the beautiful lady really did come to look at me that night when I was very small. In spite of the story being so well known, I never found anyone else who had actually seen or heard anything. But my brother and I most definitely heard that ladder and those footsteps!'

It was through the kindness of a mutual friend, Miss Joan Farrington, also of New Milton, that I met Miss Burr and had a long chat with her about her experiences and ghosts in general. She told me she did not know who presently lives in the house, known as the Old Rectory, but she always felt afraid at the house, even when she revisited it two or three years ago.

East Harptree

Some years ago now I was in correspondence with Joan Round, a journalist who had her own column in the *Daily Sketch* and she told me that she knew, first hand, about a ghost that had been seen at Coley House; and there was also a 'perfectly authentic Roundhead ghost' in the house across the road.

The previous occupants of Coley House, an elderly man, who lived there with his daughter and son-in-law, saw the ghost many times and it was heard regularly by the other members of the family. The old chap was quite accustomed to the ghost and was able to describe its dress and habits and his daughter used to hear him talking to it, although whenever she went in, she could see nothing.

When she and her husband were sitting downstairs in the evenings they would often hear footsteps coming from the old man's room: they would continue down the passage, then down an old staircase and then the couple would listen for the click of the latch

55

on the door at the foot of the stairs. The procedure was always the same: the sounds starting from the old man's room and ending with the click of the latch.

Joan Round informed me that she was told about the matter perfectly casually; they looked on the ghost as a member of the family, 'and they were not in the least an imaginative family'. Strangely enough, after the old man died, they never heard the footsteps again. Later the house changed hands and the new owner never noticed anything unusual.

Glastonbury

The George and Pilgrim Inn was built in the fifteenth century to accommodate pilgrims visiting Glastonbury Abbey and one of the bedrooms is occasionally revisited by a ghost monk, a fat and cheerful shade from the past who has been glimpsed briefly by a

The George and Pilgrim Inn: '… one of the bedrooms is revisited by a ghost monk …'

Coley Court at East Harptree.

number of people occupying the room and by members of the inn staff.

The story that is supposed to account for the ghostly appearance concerns a monk who committed suicide in the room, now known as the 'haunted cell'. One visitor described the ghost as dressed in a brown monk's habit but there was no feeling of fear associated with the experience, rather the opposite in fact, a feeling of delight and happiness.

Another visitor to the inn was awakened in the middle of the night by the sound of three light taps and when she awoke she saw the form of a man standing at the foot of her bed, smiling. By the time she had awakened her husband the figure had vanished.

An American member of the Ghost Club, during the course of a visit to Glastonbury in 1970, found himself in the centre of a curious incident. As he approached the Lady Chapel at Glastonbury he became aware of a column of white-robed figures ahead of him. Thinking that he might witness a ceremony of some kind he quickened his steps but the column of figures disappeared into what remains of the Lady Chapel before he could catch up with them. Still thinking that he would be in time to witness the event that the monks or nuns – he was not sure of the sex – were about to perform, he quickly made his way into the ruined Lady Chapel so that he would meet up with the figures he had seen only seconds before. Once inside the ruins he became aware of a strange quiet, a breathless, expectant stillness that made him feel that he was somehow caught up in a vortex. And of the column of figures there was no sign. Pulling himself together he searched everywhere. Certainly there was no time for them to have got far but he looked and looked and found nothing. They had completely disappeared and, finding himself completely alone in a world of silence, as it seemed to him, he hurriedly returned the way he had come, met up with some friends and was relieved to find himself back in the land of the living.

Higher Combe

Nearby, a few yards north of some crossroads, stands the weird and haunted Caratacus Stone.

No-one seems to know the origin of this weather-beaten and ominous-looking spur sticking up out of the ground at an angle but historians say it is probably fifth century so for something like fifteen hundred years this stone has puzzled, intrigued and frightened the people of Somerset.

A couple of hundred years ago a carter, hearing the long-standing rumours that the stone marked buried treasure, tried to uproot it with the help of his horses but the animals took fright as the stone shifted and seemed to scream. Next morning the carter was found dead, crushed by the mysterious stone.

The local people hurriedly restored the stone to its former positon and there it remains, haunted it is said on foggy nights by an apparition of frightening aspect that is both seen and heard by anyone brave enough to venture in the vicinity of the haunted stone.

Right: The Caratacus Stone is haunted on foggy nights by an apparition of frightening aspect that is both seen and heard ...

Holford, near Williton

The ancient Plough Inn here has long been haunted by the ghost of a murdered man. The story, as related to me by James Wentworth Day at a Ghost Club meeting, concerned a Spanish traveller who arrived at the inn one night in 1555, on his way to nearby Bridgwater and after an evening in the bar, when he perhaps revealed more than was wise, he climbed the outside stairway to his bedroom. At dead of night the murderer had crept up the stone stairs, quietly opened the bedroom door, and strangled to death the Spaniard as he slept; then he had stolen the traveller's money and vanished.

Today the stone steps that the murderer and the murdered climbed are no longer there but the sound of stealthy footsteps on stone steps have repeatedly been reported, at dead of night.

Mary Collier has suggested that the murder may have been political. With Mary Tudor on the throne and by no means all of her subjects approving of her liaison with Spain, the traveller may have been suspected of being a spy or on some political business and murdered accordingly.

Another version of the murder story suggests that the Spanish traveller was a wealthy merchant on his way to Bristol and believed to be carrying a hoard of gold coins with him. As he left his room and came down the outside stairway he was attacked and killed by robbers who then broke into his room, seeking the gold but they found nothing. Had the Spaniard hidden his money? If so it has not been found to this day. The ghost of the murdered man is thought, in this version of the story, to be returning periodically to make sure that his gold is still safe in its hiding place.

In 1972 the landlord, Peter Fry, told Marc Alexander that both his wife and daughter had seen the ghost of the Spanish traveller. He used to appear on the stairs where he may have been killed but after they were removed to make way for an extension, he transferred his activities to an upstairs room and it is there that he is now seen: a dark, cloaked figure. Mrs Fry saw the ghost one November night; their daughter saw the same figure one night a year later, also in November.

Right: '... haunted by the ghost of a murdered man.'

60

Nearby, the site of Walford's Gibbet is reputed to be haunted by the ghost of dark and popular John Walford, a young charcoal-burner who loved one Ann Rice. His remote occupation often took him away from Ann and a common country girl named Jenny pestered John night and day. Soon she was pregnant and John dutifully married her in June 1789 – and murdered her seventeen days later.

It is said that the judge, Lord Kenyon, wept as he sentenced John to death and faithful Ann Rice was not the only one to weep openly on the day that John was hanged by the neck until he was dead and then strung up in a cage for a year and a day as a warning to other would-be murderers.

Before he died John had a brief reunion with Ann, on his way to the scaffold, and they swore undying love for each other. Ann constantly prayed and wished with all her heart that somehow John would not suffer the agonizing death that showed in the faces of hanged men and it is a fact that John remained dignified and as handsome as ever for a week after he had been hanged.

History does not relate the fate of Ann Rice but when John's body was eventually taken down it was buried in its iron cage at the foot of the gibbet and ever since people passing by have remarked on the putrid smell of rotting flesh that hangs to this day in the air about the site of Walford's Gibbet; and sometimes, of a late summer evening, the phantom form of a handsome young man in the coarse clothes of a charcoal-burner has been encountered on the path leading away from the site of the scaffold. Is he still looking for his long dead Ann?

Locking

Locking Manor is now divided into four flats but prior to these alterations the ghost of Lady Plomley was reportedly seen on a number of occasions.

The story that may have given rise to the haunting seems to have its origin in an episode following the abortive Monmouth

Left: A haunted tree near Walford's Gibbet, where John Walford was hanged for murder.

insurrection three hundred years ago. James Scott, Duke of Monmouth (1649-1685) was the son of Lucy Walters who became the mistress of Charles II during his exile at The Hague. Today Locking Manor is owned by Lloyd Walters who tells me he has seen the ghost of Lady Plomley on two occasions; in those former restless days the squire was one John Plomley.

After the battle of Sedgemoor Monmouth's officers were rigorously hunted down and things looked bad for Plomley and his two sons who had all been sympathetic to Monmouth's cause and had in fact taken part in the ill-fated battle. Soon the two sons were caught and one was promptly hanged while the other was imprisoned but their father escaped and hid for a time in the haunted caves at Cheddar.

After a few weeks he thought the hue and cry had died down sufficiently for him to return to his home and anxious wife. Disguising himself as a peasant he made his way by a roundabout route, narrowly escaping capture on more than one occasion. Home at last he lay low but Royalist spies heard of his return and soon a troop of soldiers came to Locking Manor determined to find him. While his wife did her best to delay the soldiers, Plomley quickly hid himself in a secret hiding-place behind some panelling.

Despite his wife's protests the soldiers swarmed all over the house but they found no trace of their quarry, and they were watched by the anxious Lady Plomley, hugging her pet white spaniel in her arms for fear that he would lead the soldiers to her husband. As the angry soldiers prepared to leave the dog wriggled out of her clutches and sped like an arrow along the corridors and into the room where John Plomley was hiding: there it ran straight to the panelling hiding its master and barked excitedly at the apparently solid wall.

The wary soldiers turned and found the dog, barking and wagging its tail as it unwittingly revealed the hiding place of its master. The dog was removed and the soldiers began to methodically tap the panelling until they located a hollow sound; soon they eased back the sliding panel and discovered the hiding-place.

Realising by the sounds they made that the soldiers were on to him Plomley had sped away along the secret passage and had succeeded in reaching an out-building at Locking Head Farm half a mile away. There he had no option but to try and escape capture by hiding in a coppice but the soldiers soon surrounded him and he was captured and taken away together with Lady Plomley who had sought to hide him.

There was only one penalty and his wife was told she would be forced to watch him being hanged, drawn and quartered. She dressed herself as befitted her station and wearing the Plomley jewels, she proudly watched the dreadful sentence as it was duly carried out; and only after it was all over did she lose her composure and break down, weeping tears of frustration and unhappiness.

Back at Locking Manor she snatched up the little white spaniel that had led the soldiers to her husband, ran out into the garden and threw herself headlong down a well, taking with her the dog. Small wonder that her ghost is said to walk there and also the ghost of the little white spaniel.

During the course of some excavations some twenty years ago the original well was thought to have been discovered and when it was explored it was found to contain some forty feet of water. A complete examination has never been carried out but it is possible that there is a ledge and passageway leading off the well for neither Lady Plomley's skeleton nor her jewels have ever been found.

About the same time as the well was found a cleaner at the Manor, who knew nothing of the story or legend, shrieked with fright and rushed out of the house one morning when she encountered the shadowy form of a white spaniel in an upstairs.room; and she would never set foot in the house again.

Some fifty years ago a skeleton is said to have been discovered in the secret hiding-place behind the panelling and the secret passage was promptly sealed off at both ends; now only two steps remain to mark its position.

In August 1984 I was told that before the property was converted into flats the ghost of Lady Plomley was reportedly seen from time to time standing at the end of the passage. Mr Lloyd Walters saw it for a moment, quite clearly, before it disappeared. This happened in the early hours of the morning, between one and two o'clock. On the second occasion he saw the same figure, wearing a pointed hat with a frill and a long cloak; it glided past a basement window. Other witnesses claim to have seen a figure answering the same description and carrying a little white dog in her arms, gliding swiftly about the grounds. It has been noticed that the figure usually disappears in the vicinity of the old well.

Later, when he was in the passageway where he had seen the

ghost of Lady Plomley, Lloyd Walters saw a ghostly white spaniel running along the passage ahead of him. It has been noticed in many cases of haunting that structural alterations have resulted in the cessation of ghostly phenomena and it may be that the ghosts of Lady Plomley and her white spaniel will never again be seen at Locking Manor – on the other hand some conditions conducive to such activity may provide the atmosphere for the re-appearance of these sad ghosts.

North Petherton

Here there is a haunted piece of open roadway, a hollow, where a ghostly corpse and coffin have been reported for many years. I have before me as I write such an account dating from 1920.

Reports vary little although admittedly they are not as frequent these days when the car has long overtaken the horse as a method of transport for while horses have long been accepted as being aware of the presence of psychic activity that may be invisible to their human companions, the car is not so endowed.

Time after time travellers on horseback reported that suddenly, with an apparently clear road ahead, the horse would stop at the haunted hollow and refuse all efforts to get it going again. Occasionally a traveller would report seeing a coffin across the road with a corpse sitting on it.

The story goes that many years ago a horse fell at the hollow and broke its back. Whether the many horses who shied at the spot saw the ghost coffin that some of their human companions saw or whether they sensed the fate of the unfortunate horse that broke its back there, will, I suppose, never now be known.

Old Cleeve

Bardon House is famous as the venue of the 'Bardon Papers' indicating that the evidence contained in the 'Babington Papers',

Left: '… a traveller would see a coffin across the road with a corpse sitting on it.'

which were instrumental in causing the execution of Mary Queen of Scots, were in fact faked; but it is also famous for its ghosts: the renowned Bardon Coach, perhaps a phantom White Dove, and, formerly at any rate, the ghost of Robert Leigh.

To be exact it is the grounds of Bardon House that are haunted by the phantom coach and it is only the sound of the arrival of the vehicle that is heard these days. Incidentally the grounds are also reputed to be haunted by a headless black dog, the appearance of which was said to herald the death of a member of the Leigh family.

I am indebted to my friends and publishers Michael and Sonia Williams for a letter from Miss Joanna Cozens-Brooke who was born at Bardon House in 1898. She says: 'It is certainly haunted. I did hear that it was later known as Old Cleeve House and had become a studio ... it is a very historical house and the owners in the 1960s told

Two shots at Bardon House, renowned for a phantom coach, a white dove and the ghost of Robert Leigh.

me that letters written by Lord Darnley to Mary Queen of Scots had been found behind a panel in the attic. When I grew older my parents used to tell me grim stories of ghosts they had seen there! And the owners at that time told me about the same ghosts ... Bardon is supposed to have an underground passage to Cleeve Abbey and in the olden days many battles were fought hereabouts ...'

The famous 'White Dove of Bardon' is supposed to have been 'the spirit of the Queen' and the Bardon Papers were said to have been discovered after the dove broke a window in the room where the papers were hidden. A radio play based on the legend was broadcast some twenty years ago.

The Leigh family used to own the property and the house and grounds were long said to be haunted by the ghost of Robert Leigh but confusion seems to surround this reputed ghost for he is said to have appeared headless and to be carrying around with him a head that was not his own!

Porlock

A curious 'manifestation of the Occult' was reported several times in the neighbourhood of Porlock and the details were vouched for by a lady from Holcombe Rogus in Devon. Her evidence is based on 'a very reliable witness, a noted mason'.

One evening Mr Amos Brown was returning to his home at Porlock. The time was around ten o'clock and as he said afterwards: 'The moon was so bright you could see to pick up a pin.' He was approaching a spot where the Porlock road branched towards West Luccombe on a hill called Red Post Steep.

As Amos Brown approached Red Post he suddenly saw a lady coming towards him, every detail of her appearance clearly visible in the bright moonlight. She was apparently in evening dress: a gleaming white silk gown, patterned with dark spots; her head was bare, and her shoulder-curls fell over a falling lace collar. She was very beautiful.

As Amos Brown stood gazing at her his sole thought was amazement that such a lady should be out alone so late. Then she turned into a pathway, Old Lane, and disappeared in the direction of a ruined house.

Again, on another similar evening, William Holsworthy was passing Red Post Steep, and again the lady approached. William too was unaware of anything unusual, except that he, like Amos, was dumbfounded at the fact that so lovely a lady was walking alone so late, and he ventured to greet her: 'Good evening,' he said, and asked if he should walk with her, wherever she was going, for safety's sake.

The lady, neither answering nor apparently perceiving him, continued slowly down the slope and disappeared into the deep shadows where once stood the old house.

These are but two recorded appearances of the 'beautiful lady' but there seem to have been many manifestations of this apparition and various surmises have been hazarded for the reason for the appearance. It is possible that the Red Post was once a gallows, either permanent or temporary in time of war. Local records support this view, but the lady's described appearance does not place her too remotely in history. Possibly she dates from the Civil War, when there were fierce skirmishes around these parts so near Dunster; and the lady's falling collar and curls point to this supposition. But the clearest detail of all, the spotted silk of her gown, does not seem to allow of any very early date, although spotted materials were always obtainable, apparently, from the Orient and were in fact imported by the East Indian Company early in their history.

That the spots were the clearest evidence of all, and were noticed by all, is beyond question. The lady was seen on so many occasions, and her appearance became such a recurring event that children would ask of their parents: 'Have you seen the lovely Lady in the Spotted Dress?'

Sedgemoor

The early days of July 1685 saw the sad and sorry battle of Sedgemoor with James, Duke of Monmouth, leading a mob of brave Englishmen against the well-armed British Regulars; a battle that robbed England of some twelve hundred men, the last battle fought on English soil.

The followers of popular but bungling Monmouth were fighting for an ideal but they were armed with makeshift weapons and were no match for the expert artillery of the encamped Royalist army. The slaughter on both sides was dreadful although the battle lasted only a few hours. Perhaps it was the emotional element in the conflict; perhaps it was the frightful carnage; perhaps the singular atmosphere pervading the flat field that early summer morning – whatever it was something remains at Sedgemoor to remind us of that wet, sad day.

Ghostly remnants of Monmouth's brave army have been encountered at King's Sedgemoor Drain and many are the stories hereabouts of phantom soldiers, ragged and weary, wandering about the marshy battlefield. Sometimes voices are heard and the distant roar of hand-to-hand fighting, and the faint call of 'Come on over!'

Alasdair Alpin MacGregor told me about Mr and Mrs Horace Robinson who were motoring across Sedgemoor when they suddenly found themselves in the midst of strangely attired and oddly armed fighting men. Their son Philip recalled that his mother often related her experience and remembered telling her husband to stop the car for fear of running into the people carrying staves and

pikes ... then, as suddenly as they had appeared, the phantom men disappeared.

Charles Hugh Rose, Jimmy Wentworth Day's childhood tutor, told him that on one occasion he was driving in the area when he encountered a ghost cavalier on horseback. Rose clearly saw every detail of the figure's face and uniform and was utterly convinced that he had seen the ghost of Monmouth himself. The date was 3 July and every year on that date the phantom form of Monmouth is said to appear, making no sound, as he repeats his escape from the battlefield (notwithstanding that the date of the battle was 6 July).

Another ghost at Sedgemoor is that of a girl who committed suicide. The story goes that she had a sweetheart who followed Monmouth, an athlete renowned for his running, and when he was captured by the Royalist soldiers he was told that if he could run as fast as a galloping horse his life would be spared.

The desperate man, frantic to live, managed to keep pace with a cavalry rider but the watching girl's joy turned to unbearable sadness when the exhausted runner was shot anyway. The weeping girl ran away from the sight of her dead lover and drowned herself near the battlefield and her sad phantom has haunted the place ever since, accompanied by the drumming of horses' hooves and the strained panting sounds of a running man.

Some years ago there was a lot of correspondence in local and national papers concerning apparitions on Sedgemoor and in particular a 'sheeted rider' that seems to have been seen on many occasions. Mention is made of a seventeenth century chap-book which gives a detailed account of an apparition seen on Monday, 22 September 1690 by a Mr Jacob Seley who related the full story of his experience the next day to the judges of the Western Circuit.

Sax Rohmer told me that he had obtained a great deal of evidence for apparitions on Sedgemoor and he referred to the matter in one of his books saying, '... the unhappy Duke and some of his staff have been seen on stormy nights, crossing the path which skirts the moor.'

Luke Speedwell, during the course of a tour of England by car in 1924 said: 'You will not be ready to believe what I have next to record, but it is a fact. As we forged through the fog I suddenly

Left: '... stories of phantom soldiers ...'

beheld right ahead a horseman riding a white horse. As we drew near I could see that the horse was of a big and heavy breed. The rider was clothed in flowing white. It was well past midnight. I slowed down and hailed the rider. There was no response and I then noticed that his horse's hooves made no sound. He passed, in complete silence, never turning his head and at last horse and rider vanished into the moor.'

A Mr J. Staples of Cambridge contributed to the correspondence to say that the sheeted rider at midnight on Sedgemoor was 'one of the few authentic ghosts in England'. He added that the appearance of this spectre had been vouched for again and again and that his tutor – a Somerset man – swore that he had seen it. Mr Staples sent to the editor of the *Daily Express* the names of a rector and a bishop, both of whom said they had seen the ghostly sheeted rider.

Shepton Mallet Prison: '… a white lady who is thought to have been beheaded here.'

Shepton Mallet

The grim prison here, more than three centuries old and a notorious Army 'glasshouse' until 1966, is reputed to be haunted by a female figure, a White Lady who is thought to have been beheaded here in 1680.

In 1967 I went there following a spate of reports of unaccountable banging sounds, noises that sounded like heavy breathing, the feeling that 'someone or something invisible was in one room', an oppressive, overbearing feeling and an icy chilling atmosphere that frightened those using the night duty room.

Such reports became so numerous that the prison governor spent a night in the 'haunted' room himself and sent a full report to the Home Office. There was no doubt that apparently inexplicable things were taking place and the governor reported: 'I was unable to find any satisfactory explanation for the happenings.'

The governor then asked the chaplain's Prebendary Leonard White and Father Ryan to speak to the worried staff and one of the senior wardens told me: 'Prebendary White told us to try to forget the incidents but it isn't easy when you've had this kind of experience. We are all scared stiff and nobody has yet come up with an explanation.'

I talked with another prison officer who said he had suddenly experienced an icy feeling on the back of his neck and had the frightening sensation that somebody invisible was pushing from the other side when he was trying to lock a door, although in fact nobody was there. He also once had the very unpleasant feeling of being pinned down by the neck and a paralysed sensation lasted in his neck throughout the whole of one night. This particular officer had not entered the night duty room since that experience. Yet another officer admitted, somewhat reluctantly it is true, that he had seen a white shape that could have been a female form but when he went closer it vanished.

The attitude of practically the whole of the prison staff at that time was summed up for me by one warder who stated: 'I wouldn't spend another night in the duty room for £1000.' Later the Home Office told me: 'All is now quiet there.'

As recently as November 1984 some inmates of the jail built on the site of a wartime gallows claimed that they were being haunted by

one of the people hanged there. Some of the witnesses said the form was dressed in Second World War uniform and appeared in the Library of the prison. The Home Office confirmed at the time that the Library is built on the site of a Death Row used by the Americans during the war and by Albert Pierrepoint, Britain's last hangman; but on the subject of the ghost sightings they said, 'We do not intend to do anything about that.'

Nearby Cannard's Grave Inn stands at the intersection of five roads and the inn sign is a gibbet with a hanged man. The inn takes its name from a seventeenth-century innkeeper named Giles Cannard who is said to have made a fortune from his dealings with highwaymen and smugglers. Still not satisfied he tried his hand at forgery but he was found out and when he knew the game was up, rather than submit to the law, he hanged himself and was buried at the crossroads where once his gang of footpads would lie in wait for solitary travellers. From time to time his ghost still frightens travellers to this area on dark wintry nights.

Sparkford

There used to be an ancient causeway running between nearby South and North Barrow where each Midsummer's Eve the ghosts of King Arthur and his knights were said to ride, accompanied by foot soldiers whose spears and lances are tipped with flames ... Not far away Arthur's Hunting Causeway is reputedly haunted each Christmas Eve by the same King Arthur and his knights, their steeds silver-shod; and not too long ago a silver horseshoe was reportedly found on the ancient trackway!

The eminent folklorist Christina Hole told me that she had spoken with a woman who, in the 1920s, had watched a line of bright lights move along a nearby trackway. As they came nearer she saw they were a troop of armed warriors carrying flame-tipped lances and led by an impressive mounted figure. They made no sound and then, suddenly, they were no longer there.

The hill known as Cadbury Castle is as likely to have been the site

Left: The inn sign is a gibbet with a hanged man whose ghost still frightens travellers.

of King Arthur's Camelot as anywhere and it is small wonder that claims to have seen the ghosts of the legendary King and his knights have frequently been reported here although legend has it that they ride out of the hill only once every seven years.

As more than one writer has pointed out the whole area round Cadbury and the deep lanes surrounding it have a strangely evocative atmosphere; a place where the barriers between this world and the next are weakest.

Stogumber

A village that has long had the reputation of being haunted by the Wild Hunt: Woden on his white horse leads the hunt and brings death and disaster to all who watch him pass. Through the streets here the Wild Hunt is said to race and there are those who claim to have heard it in 1960 but none dared look when they heard the fearful sounds.

Nearby for centuries stood the Heddon Oak, at the junction of two lanes. Here the mutilated bodies of some of Monmouth's men were hanged and left to swing in the wind as a warning to others. The Hanging Tree, as it was called, was cut down in 1979 but the site remains haunted.

People passing this way have experienced a sudden feeling that they are choking; others have heard the sounds of groans and clanking chains, or of hoofbeats, creaking leather and heavy breathing, followed by strangling noises. It can be a weird place after nightfall, somewhere to be avoided by man and beast.

Taunton

Historic Taunton was founded by King Ina twelve centuries ago and from the strong castle he built there he dominated all England south of London, the first Saxon ruler with such power and unity.

Here Geoffrey Chaucer's son Thomas was once Constable and in

Left: 'The ghosts of King Arthur and his knights were said to ride ...'

the Civil War there was stiff and bloody fighting; but it is the name of Judge Jeffreys that is forever linked with Taunton for here he held the Assizes after the fall of Monmouth who had been proclaimed King Monmouth when he had ridden into the town. Indeed Judge Jeffreys's room at the Tudor Tavern here is reputed to be haunted by his restless presence; and an impressive bewigged figure has been seen standing on a landing of the castle museum. This is thought to be the infamous judge who is probably the best remembered black figure in history and the commonest ghost in Somerset.

The Duke and his army occupied the castle and the present Castle Hotel, once part of the great castle, is now haunted periodically, not by a rowdy soldier but by a gentle lady violinist or perhaps a fiddler who has been seen but more frequently heard and not seen, in the apartment known as the Fiddlers' Room. Here, too, at least one visitor to a certain bedroom has found herself suddenly wide awake in the middle of the night to hear soft movement around the foot of her bed followed by the sensation of a hand gently smoothing the bedclothes ...

A museum occupies another section of the old castle and here the tramping sound of invisible boots have been reported; heavy dragging sounds that may have their origin in the days when the rebel soldiers were dragged into the Great Hall to face the wrath of the Hanging Judge. Here, too, some years ago, the then Curator claimed on one occasion to see a pair of disembodied ghostly hands and on another day he encountered the figure of a fair-haired young lady in seventeenth-century dress – a figure which disappeared almost as soon as he became aware of its presence.

The old castle is also said to be haunted by the ghost of a cavalier who has been seen on a stairway landing, a frightening and menacing figure in high boots holding a pistol in one hand and a sword in the other.

The Crescent at Taunton has long been haunted by the ghost of an elderly lady dressed in black silk and wearing black mittens. Who she is no-one knows for whenever she has been addressed, those seeing her taking her for a real person, she never answers and soon disappears but historians think she may be Mrs Maria Anne Fitzherbert, the morganatic wife of George IV.

Left: Woden on his white horse leads the hunt.

A correspondent, Mrs Frances Veale, tells me that her sister-in-law used to live at the Old Toll House (now demolished) and she had many ghostly experiences there. She and others used to see a lady attired in old-fashioned hunting dress gliding up and down the stairs and sometimes a phantom goose waddled along the stone corridor leading to the old dairy where it disappeared!

Tolland

Gaulden, a small manor of great charm has a history that goes back some seven hundred years. It is a house associated with the Turberville family, immortalised by Thomas Hardy, and the house has the reputation of having had visits from the phantom coach of the Turbervilles; such visits supposedly presaged the death of a member of the family and, as Mr and Mrs James Le Gendre Starkie told me when I was there in the autumn of 1984, since there were no longer any Turbervilles at Gaulden Manor, it no longer has a phantom coach either – but it has other ghosts.

James Turberville, a Bishop of Exeter who refused to take the Oath of Supremacy to Elizabeth I in 1559, was imprisoned in the Tower of London with five other like-minded bishops but in 1563 he was released and allowed to spend the last years of his life quietly at Gaulden. Some authorities believe that the splendid plaster frieze round the Great Hall tells the story of the life and times of the bishop. Over the great fireplace in the Hall are the arms of the Turberville of Bere Regis and on either side the arms of forbears of James Turberville, Sir Robert and Sir Richard Turberville: can the heavy footsteps on the main stairway, that have been heard so many times, be those of James Turberville who must have come to love this lovely house?

Outside, Mrs Starkie showed my wife and I the Bog Garden, the Elizabethan Herb Garden and the haunted Bishop's Garden. Here a number of monks are supposed to have been buried and this is likely since Gaulden was in the possession of Taunton Priory in the twelfth century; the large pond in the grounds doubtless providing the

Right: The site of Heddon Oak where some of Monmouth's men were hung.

monks with their fish – and in the Bishop's Garden ghost monks have been seen on many occasions in the past.

I found lots of snippets of mystery at Gaulden Manor: the story of a secret passage that is supposed to run towards Wiveliscombe, and another secret passage towards the old buildings at Grove Farm where there was once a nunnery; numerous stories of strange happenings that the local people have related to Mr and Mrs Starkie; the identity of the ghost of a small woman who haunts the front stairs, and the ghostly grey lady who sits on the righthand side of the fireplace. In 1982 a visitor told the present owners that when he worked at Gaulden the owner at that time always kept one room locked and shuttered because it was so haunted by a ghostly lady that it saved too many questions being asked.

Off the Great Hall there is a small room that has always been called the Chapel, divided from the Hall by beautiful carved panels. Late in the autumn afternoon, when we were there, my wife sat alone in the Great Hall for a while and when Mrs Starkie asked her whether she liked the room, my wife said she felt something very unpleasant had happened in the area of the carved panels and only then did Mrs Starkie recall that once a visitor, about to enter the Hall for the first time, said he could see three cavaliers standing in front of the carved panels, covered in blood; and he refused to enter the room at all. Another visitor, a responsible schoolmaster, also finds something very frightening about the Great Hall and it is a fact that there was a battle near Gaulden during the Civil War and it is very probable that some cavaliers were here, perhaps badly wounded, perhaps dying, and that they have left behind something that some people can detect three hundred years later. Cromwell's men were at Gaulden Manor for over a week on one occasion.

Twice in 1967 the present owners heard loud and distinct knocks on the door at the head of the stairs. On each occasion there were just two sharp knocks in the middle of the night, loud enough to awaken both Mr and Mrs Starkie. Nothing was found to account for the knocks. It was here, at the top of the stairs, and without knowing anything about the mysterious knocks, that a visitor in 1983 suddenly stopped and said the hair at the back of his neck prickled and he was sure something terrible had happened there.

Left: The ghost of a cavalier has been seen ...

Three cavaliers covered in blood ...

Twice too Mr and Mrs Starkie have heard footsteps mounting the main staircase, very loud and distinct footsteps, but there is never any sound continuing beyond the top of the stairs and nothing has ever been found to account for the sounds.

The room at the top of the stairs, the Turberville Bedroom, seemed to me to be a happy room but my wife immediately said she did not like the room and later we learned that it was here that an old housekeeper said she had seen the ghost of a monk. We talked with Mrs Hunter, who helps in the house and in the shop when the house is open to the public, and with her daughter: both have seen ghosts at Gaulden Manor and strange to relate Mrs Hunter may have seen a ghost on the day that we were there!

On Thursday, 18 October 1984, my wife and I arrived at Gaulden Manor about eleven o'clock in the morning as required by Jeremy Mills, the producer of 'Slade Alive' for the purpose of a day's filming for television. After a few moments my wife left to explore some of the antique shops of the area and returned to collect me about 3.30 p.m. Almost as soon as she was inside the house Mrs Hunter asked her whether she had changed and returned to Gaulden Manor at lunch time, which of course she had not done, but Mrs Hunter said she had been working in the dining room and had looked up around noon and had seen a lady with dark hair and wearing a blue costume of some sort standing in the hall by the front door; after a moment the figure was no longer there. My wife's dark hair and her general size suggested to Mrs Hunter that she was the only real person it could have been, the only person at Gaulden Manor that day who looked anything like the figure she saw but my wife was miles away at the time.

The present owners find the house to have a pleasant and warm atmosphere and if there are still ghosts there they believe they are friendly ones but it seems certain that ghosts have been seen at beautiful Gaulden Manor in the past and perhaps they will be seen again.

Twerton

Six occupants of a council house here claimed, in 1975, to see on three successive nights, the ghostly figure of an old man 'with a horrible wrinkled skin'. The form, 'big and black', didn't seem to have a face and one wonders just how authentic the story was for I never managed to obtain a firsthand account of the events or discover any history of the council house or anything about a property that had previously occupied the site that might have lent credence to the reported sightings. And yet, who but those who were there at the time and experienced the event can really say?

Watchet

The Wyndham family lived for a time at nearby haunted Kentsford Farm near the church where there is a brass of two Elizabethan members of the family, John and Florence Wyndham – and a strange story has been handed down concerning this Florence Wyndham.

It is said that as she lay in her coffin awaiting burial the sexton, coveting her rings, broke open the coffin to find her alive! Back home she soon gave birth to the son whose portrait appears with his wife's on another ancient brass in this fifteenth-century church.

It is probably a variation of this story that Elliott O'Donnell recounted at a Ghost Club meeting. He told of a local schoolmaster, passing the church late one night, encountering some shady characters who asked him to point out to them where a certain rich lady had recently been buried. The schoolmaster at first refused to answer but when the ruffians began to threaten him he became very frightened and he showed them the crypt.

Here the men produced iron bars and having removed the grille, forced open the door and pushed the schoolmaster through the opening, telling him to open the new coffin inside and bring them the seven rings he would find on the fingers of the corpse. Terrified by the attitide of the thugs, the schoolmaster proceeded to do as he had been asked and he obtained six of the rings and was pulling off the last one when the corpse suddenly sat up and cried out! At this some of the other coffins in the crypt burst open and the waiting robbers, hearing the commotion, fled. The schoolmaster, frightened out of his wits by this time, ran up the steps into the church and hid himself in the choir. Frightening, ghostly forms seemed to follow him and taking up a pole he frantically pushed them away until midnight struck, whereupon the ghosts or whatever they were, turned tail and disappeared back into the crypt.

As soon as he felt it was safe to do so the schoolmaster fled home, feeling very weak and ill after this ordeal. Next day, still terribly shocked by the experience and feeling no better, he sent for the rector of the parish and told him all that had happened. A few days later the schoolmaster was dead.

Within recent years tappings at the window of the dining room and the ghostly figure of a lady on the stairs of the farmhouse have been attributed to the ghost of Florence Wyndham.

Perhaps the earliest ghost here is that of St Decuman, to whom the church is dedicated, for legend has it that he was set upon by a local pagan who cut off the saint's head as he knelt at his devotions and his decapitated body is said to have raised itself, lifted its head in its hands, and carried it to a spot nearby where, when he was alive, the saint was in the habit of washing. Today that spot is marked by a 'holy well'.

Be that as it may the most recent ghostly happenings here are the

The big, black form didn't seem to have a face.

sounds of Edwardian children riding to their holidays and a phantom train; modern ghosts that haunt the long disused railway lines.

Some forty years ago now three men have related how they watched a train chugging slowly towards the bridge on which they kept vigil for several hours on successive nights. They were astonished by what they all saw for the railway track had been closed for more than thirty years. Stories of the phantom train were fast becoming part of Westcountry folklore although it was still possible at that time to talk with people who claimed that on still nights the sound of the ghost train could be heard several miles away; others maintained that they had seen the glow from the engine's firebox moving slowly along the overgrown embankment.

The three men, two lived locally, a postman and an agricultural worker, and the third who was a psychical researcher, spent five bitterly cold February nights waiting for the ghost train and on the sixth night they said their patience was rewarded. Along the single curved track steamed a tank engine pulling a line of trucks. The bridge upon which the men stood was little used and led to abandoned brickworks. When the men told their stories they were met with such cynicism that they went to a solicitor to swear an affidavit confirming what they had seen.

The researcher first became interested in the story soon after the Second World War when a friend sent him some notes on the case compiled by a local historian; the postman and his friend said they took a short cut over the bridge after band practice late one night and both of them saw a train and trucks coming along the line. Just as the train was about to pass under the bridge it vanished. The two men were reluctant to talk about their experience but eventually their stories were reported in a local paper and several dozen people then wrote in to say that they too had heard or seen the ghost train or knew someone who had.

The researcher went to see the two men, satisfied himself that they were good witnesses, and it was arranged that they would all three spend a few nights keeping watch for the arresting spectacle. After five nights the researcher was prepared to abandon the project

Left: Stories of the phantom train were fast becoming part of Westcountry folklore.

but the other two persuaded him to try for one more night and just before midnight they all saw a locomotive and about six mineral trucks heading down the line towards them. They could see the glow of the fire and the shape of a steam locomotive; all that was missing was the noise. The train, running at about 20 m.p.h., was completely silent. As it approached the bridge the researcher braced himself for further developments as the train passed beneath him and momentarily he closed his eyes. When he opened them again the train had vanished and everything had returned to normal. He wondered whether he had imagined the whole episode until his companions described in detail exactly what he had himself seen. Several further watches were subsequently arranged but no more sightings of the ghost train were recorded.

It is interesting to relate that a history of the West Somerset Mineral Railway records a bad accident in 1857 between two trains, one carrying about thirty labourers returning to Watchet for their pay and travelling about 20 m.p.h. and the other a coal train proceeding out of Watchet. They collided head on as they rounded a corner at Kentsford and three men were killed and a number injured. Many of the rails here were ripped up in 1917; others remain rusting, weed-choked and still haunted by the sound of laughing children and not so long ago by a phantom train.

Wells

The King Charles Hotel here, dating from medieval days, is reputedly haunted by the ghost of a cavalier; the sound of a harpsichord and the sound of heavy footsteps.

In 1978 the former manageress stated that she had seen the cavalier ghost several times on the old staircase. On chancing to mention the incident to the cellarman, who had known the hotel for years, she was told that such a figure had been seen many times and always on the stairs.

Some years later, the Hanson's young son told his parents that he had seen a 'pretty man' at the top of the stairway and on one occasion Philip Hanson heard what he described as 'the sound of a

Left: King Charles Hotel haunted by a cavalier.

93

harpsichord coming from nowhere'. Another night he and his wife Ann heard the sound of heavy footsteps that seemed to come from the top of the Jacobean stairs. On yet another occasion Philip distinctly felt 'something' brush past him as he was ascending the same stairs.

In September 1984 I asked the present owners whether they had had any odd experiences and Jules Gardner told me, 'We only purchased the hotel in April of this year but we were told at the time that we had acquired a ghost along with the fixtures and fittings!' Local people told them a ghostly cavalier frequented the passage-ways and the back staircase but so far, I was told, 'we have neither seen him nor heard him or had any strange occurrences at all . . . but if we should see or hear anything, I will be only too happy to pass it on to you ...' I look forward to looking in at the King Charles Hotel the next time I am in Wells.

'Gournay Court was very haunted at one time ...'

The Old Vicarage at West Harptree.

West Harptree

Margaret Royal, who has made a study of the ghosts and hauntings in the Bath and Bristol areas, tells me that Gournay Court was very haunted at one time, although neither the present nor the previous owners have heard or seen anything unusual.

During the First World War the place was used as a convalescent home for wounded soldiers and at that time the apparition of a man in a velvet suit with knee breeches and wearing stockings and shoes with large buckles, used to be seen by the soldiers and staff, usually coming down the main stairway and passing through the ballroom.

The Old Vicarage here used to have a ghost that most frequently appeared at the bottom of the stairs. The then vicar repeatedly told his parishioners of seeing the phantom and said he was terrified of it and as often as he could he arranged for someone to enter the house with him when he was out late. One night he returned to the vicarage unaccompanied and the following morning a tradesman noticed the vicar's milk was still on his doorstep. He and some neighbours broke into the house and found the vicar dead at the foot of the stairs, in the exact spot where he always said he saw the ghost.

Nearby the ruins of Richmont Castle have long been said to be haunted; some say by the ghost of a man in a long cloak and black hat, and others say by a knight, but at all events he is thought to be a member of the Gournay family who once owned the castle. There is a story that in revenge for the 'unfortunate condition' of a young female member of the family, the young heir challenged a 'tall, dark stranger' to a duel but the stranger won and the innocent Gournay sometimes returns to the spot where he breathed his last and waits, silent and apprehensive, for his adversary to show up, as he must have waited, long years ago. Once, a labourer, on his way home late from work, encountered what he described as 'a dark knight', a ghostly form that seemed to say to him: 'It is past midnight and time you left this place to whom it belongs!' Perhaps understandably the labourer never went that way again after midnight.

Weston-super-Mare

Mrs A. Barwood of Hastings tells me that she had a ghostly experience at Weston-super-Mare hospital after the birth of her last baby, when she had to stay in hospital for two months. On account of her condition she was placed alone in a separate ward. Late one night, when all was quiet, she found herself suddenly wide awake. She had always insisted on her door being left open and a light burned all night in the corridor outside. As she lay wondering what had awakened her, she looked round to see a lady in a blue dressing gown coming along the corridor towards her room, apparently looking at herself in a hand mirror.

She knew that the person in the ward across the hall had gone home that day and at first nothing seemed unnatural but then the figure entered the ward and reached the bedside of my informant. Quite suddenly Mrs Barwood found that she was sweating profusely and was very frightened. The form did not speak but quietly backed away from the bed, out of the room, across the corridor and right through the closed door of the ward opposite! Only then did Mrs Barwood realise that she must be seeing a ghost!

Next morning she insisted on going home although she did not reveal to the nursing sister the reason why she could not spend another night in the ward. Writing many years after the event Mrs Barwood said she never forgot the experience and she had often wondered whether anyone else had seen a similar ghost at the hospital.

In 1973 I learned about a nurse at the same hospital who recounted several puzzling experiences. Soon after going on night duty, when she had been at the hospital only a short time, she entered a small ward and saw a nurse in a blue dress bending over a patient. She looked at her watch, wondering who it could be and seeing that the time was just after 1.30 a.m., she decided it must be the night superintendent of the hospital making an unannounced round of the patients; when she looked again there was no sign of the figure!

Puzzled, she entered the ward and discovered that there was no other way out, simply the one door by which she had entered and she established without a shadow of a doubt that the nurse in blue was no longer in the small ward. Still very puzzled the young nurse went over to the patient occupying the ward and found he was a young soldier, crying quietly. He was recovering from the complaint for which he was in hospital but seemed very depressed and the nurse said she would fetch him a cup of tea. While she was making the tea in the duty room the soldier walked in and said he was very unhappy and would like to talk to her.

They sat down with the tea and he told her that he had just heard that his mother had died and he had been told that he had tuberculosis and would have to leave the Army. Without really knowing what made her say it, the young nurse found herself comforting the unhappy soldier and saying: 'Your T.B. is curable. You will be sent to a convalescent home; you will be cured and you will be happy. Your mother will always be near you ...'

In due course the soldier was transferred to a sanatorium but he wrote to the nurse from time to time. Some three years later he wrote to say that he had been pronounced cured, he had married and was going to live in New Zealand. He added, 'I wonder whether you recall that time you found me awake and unhappy? When I opened my eyes and saw you bending over me, there was another nurse behind you, dressed in blue; when you straightened up and said you would get some tea, the other figure disappeared – that's why I came to the duty room. I didn't tell you at the time because I thought you might be frightened ... after I left the hospital I discovered that a nurse in blue frequently visited patients who were sad. She seems to be a ghost of good omen, for those to whom she appeared invariably recovered ...'

Wookey Hole

When Mrs Olive Hodgkinson owned Wookey Hole – her husband's family had owned the cave for generations – she told me there was no possible doubt but that the place was haunted. I talked to her in a haunted cottage on the Wookey estate.

The Great Cave, formed by the River Axe thousands of years ago, was occupied by primitive man more than two thousand years ago – it is in fact the oldest known home of man in Britain – and it is said that it was first recorded in the second century after Christ. Its best known inhabitant is the Witch: according to archaeologists, repeatedly pacified by human sacrifices and eventually petrified; according to legend, it was once a brave monk from Glastonbury.

The story goes that the witch was once as beautiful to look upon as she was powerful in the black arts, but she became old before her time and when she was hunched and ugly, twisted and toothless, the sight of young lovers hand in hand maddened her for with all her knowledge and experience she could not bring back her own beauty. One day as a pair of lovers lingered near her, full of love and with eyes only for each other, the witch became demented with rage and vowed to break the love the couple shared.

Working in a frenzy, conjuring up evil spirits, using all her means to harness the powers of darkness, she soon succeeded in her plans and the couple parted. The young man, heartbroken at being parted from his one and only love, turned his back on the world and became a monk at Glastonbury Abbey.

When he learned that it was the work of the evil witch of Wookey Hole that had destroyed his love, he set about combating the forces of evil and with his Abbot's blessing he set out to defeat the witch with a cross of holy wood and a phial of holy water. When the witch showed herself the young man threw the holy water in her face, raised the wooden cross and prayed as he had never prayed before. In front of his eyes the witch, after uttering one last terrible scream, turned to stone and her black, misshapen form can still seen.

Such a tale with its ingredients of transformation into stone and the triumph of good over evil was regarded for centuries as a convenient legend to account for the odd shape of the age-old stalactite but in 1912 excavation uncovered parts of the skeleton of a very ancient female and beside the remains lay a dagger, a knife, a weaving comb, the bones of two goats, and a white ball-like object that could have once been a witch ball – or more accurately, a watch ball for such balls were often used for scrying.

The cottage where Olive Hodgkinson told me about Wookey Hole and its ghosts was built in 1878 and was occupied for over sixty years by a dear old lady who died in the cottage in 1947. She had always refused to have electricity but it was installed after her death when her husband and son had left. Then odd happenings began to take place.

A young couple with an eight-year-old boy moved in temporarily and one evening the boy came down the stairs and said he had seen an old lady in a white apron upstairs. His mother immediately went upstairs and herself saw the ghost of an old lady crossing the landing. Soon the frequent alleged sightings of the ghost and unexplained footsteps up and down the stairs drove the family out. Olive Hodgkinson found other tenants complained not only of the ghost and the footsteps but also of doors opening and closing by themselves and before long the cottage stood empty and deserted.

In the 1950s, when the disturbances at the cottage were at their height, Olive Hodgkinson arranged for a psychic investigator to sit up with her for the whole of one night in the cottage; they did so but saw no ghost. It had been noted that cats and dogs showed a marked aversion to entering the cave and an even greater aversion to passing the so-called Witch of Wookey and wondering whether her cats would exhibit any signs of being aware of unseen disturbances at the cottage Olive Hodgkinson took her two cats into the cottage to watch their behaviour. One of them curled up in a chair and was soon asleep while the other seemed terrified of something and sat awake all night, never closing her eyes for a moment. I told Olive Hodgkinson that I had noted long ago that while all dogs seem to be super-sensitive, cats are like human beings and some are seemingly aware of psychic happenings and some are not.

**St Mary the Virgin Church
at Yatton.**

At five o'clock in the morning both the investigator and Olive Hodgkinson thought they heard a movement but before they could do anything the sleeping cat was wide awake and she sprang out of her chair and leapt on to the window ledge, her back arched, while the other wide-awake cat shot out of the room with her hackles high.

Mrs Hodgkinson's manageress at the time was highly sceptical of the whole business of ghosts and she readily agreed to sleep in the vacant cottage. As soon as she moved in she expressed a feeling of unease, an extraordinary feeling which she found most unpleasant and which prevented her from getting proper rest and sleep at night. At about two a.m. she started up in terror when she felt the unmistakable touch of a cold hand on her shoulder, and she saw the ghostly form of a female walk through the bedroom door.

Next morning she said she knew for the first time in her life precisely what it was like to say one's hair stood on end; she was white and drawn and completely shattered. She would never spend another night at the cottage.

Mrs Hodgkinson's chef, when he took a turn at the cottage, complained that he had spent a sleepless night, the most unpleasant night of his life, in the so-called haunted bedroom and he also complained of a dreadful, dead smell which came and went in waves and for which no natural explanation was ever found. Things became so bad that the cottage was blessed by the vicar of Wookey in 1954 but still the disturbances were not halted. One member of the staff said she awoke in the middle of the night to see a figure walk through the wall into the bedroom where it vanished.

Olive Hodgkinson told me that the disturbances continued for nearly five years and she produced for me evidence from twenty-three people who had experienced the disturbances in one form or another, seven of them claiming to have seen the ghost. Gradually the disturances became less frequent, I was told, and eventually ceased altogether.

In 1981 members of the Wessex Caving Club were completely mystified by strange noises and flashing lights during excavations in some of the pot-holes here and they obtained tape-recordings of the sounds. In addition to regular tapping sounds there was also a dragging noise, almost as though someone was painfully crawling along the tunnel. 'It was most eerie,' the cavers said at the time, 'for no human can ever have been there because the cave was blocked by sand and gravel for two million years.'

During the course of a television programme in 1982 John Hedges said: 'The mysteries of Wookey Hole remain still unsolved.' How right he is.

Yatton

A lovely place full of old houses and picturesque corners and with a church that has parts that go back seven hundred years. Inside you can see a tiny stone figure of St Margaret slaying a dragon; some lovely ladies' heads with fashionable head-dresses and some with strange, distorted features. One of the loveliest corners of the church is the Chapel of St John the Evangelist with its tomb of Sir John Newton and his wife and St John's Chapel is, or was, haunted.

In 1952 two of the church dignitaries, the vicar's warden and the organist, claimed they saw a grey-robed ghostly figure inside the church. Mr T.L. Harbourne, the warden, said that while he was arranging collecting bags one afternoon, he saw the grey-robed figure of a lady walk slowly from the direction of the altar. Her head, he said, was bent and her hands were clasped, as if in prayer. 'She walked slowly between the choir stalls and passed round the pillar and into St John's Chapel,' Mr Harbourne told me at the time. 'I went to speak to her and suddenly found myself alone. I recall that she wore a close-fitting cap on her head and a veil hung halfway down her back.'

Mr H.B. Emery, who told me he had been organist at St Mary's for twenty-six years, said he had seen the same figure on three occasions. It was, he thought, a tall lady, wearing a grey robe and she moved across the aisle towards St John's Chapel without making any sound. He pointed out to me the carving of Lady Isobel Newton inside the chapel; a tall figure, loosely robed and wearing over her head a veil-like ornament reaching down her back. Lady Isobel died in 1498.

Yeovil

In Middle Street in the town centre the Elephant and Castle Inn is reputed to be haunted by the ghost of an unknown female, dressed in a long white gown, who carries a lamp. The landlady some years ago was Mrs Sword and she told me she had seen the figure several times. 'She wears a long gown and some sort of head covering,' she said. 'And she carries a lamp or maybe it is a candle. We think she must be a maid who lived and worked here at one time; she certainly makes a lot of noise on occasions – sounds like crockery and cutlery being stacked and moved but we've never found anything to account for the sounds.'

Several visitors who have had no knowledge that the inn has a ghost have reported seeing a similar figure. One man described the figure he saw as being that of a girl of about twenty-four, wearing a long white gown and having a head-dress that hid most of her hair and carrying a lamp or tall candle. He saw this form on suddenly awakening in his bedroom about five o'clock one morning. She seemed to disappear through the wardrobe but in fact probably disappeared through the wall at the spot where the wardrobe stood. Another visitor said she saw a similar figure in the same bedroom; a small person in a long dress and holding a lamp of some sort. In common with many genuine ghosts, in Somerset and elsewhere, one moment she was there and the next she had gone.

Acknowledgments

In addition to the many historians, librarians, editors and friends throughout the county of Somerset who have been good enough to assist with information for this volume the author would like to especially mention Mrs C. Baker, Mrs A. Barwood, Miss Chili Bouchier, Miss Cynthia Burr, H.B. Emery, Miss Joan Farrington, Mrs C.A. Feeney, Jules M. Gardner, T.L. Harbourne, Mrs Olive Hodgkinson, Mrs and Miss Hunter, Air Commodore R.C. Jonas, Mrs Doreen Jones, Miss Joan Round, Mrs Margaret Royal, Deryck Seymour, Mr and Mrs James Le Gendre Starkie, Mrs Frances Veale, Lloyd Walters, Peter Welch and in particular his publishers and friends Sonia and Michael Williams.

Select Bibliography

Alexander, Marc, *Haunted Inns*, 1973; *Phantom Britain*, 1975; *Haunted Churches and Abbeys of Britain*, 1978

Brown, Raymond Lamont, *A Casebook of Military Mystery*, 1974

Christian, Roy, *Ghosts and Legends*, 1972

Cox, Antony D. Hippisley, *Haunted Britain*, 1973

Green, Andrew, *Our Haunted Kingdom*, 1973; *Ghosts of Today*, 1980

Hole, Christina, *Haunted England*, 1940

Hallam, Jack, *The Haunted Inns of England*, 1972

Harries, John, *The Ghost Hunter's Road Book*, 1968

Jones, Sally, *Legends of Somerset*, 1984

Lawrence, Berta, *Somerset Legends*, 1973

Legg, Collier and Perrott, *Ghosts of Dorset, Devon and Somerset*, 1974

MacGregor, Alasdair Alpin, *Phantom Footsteps*, 1959

O'Donnell, Elliott, *Haunted Churches*, 1939

Mee, Arthur, Somerset: *The King's England*, 1968 ed.

Poole, Keith B., *Ghosts of Wessex*, 1976

Royal, Margaret and Girvan, Ian, *Local Ghosts*, 1976; *Bristol Ghosts*, 1977

Sellick, Roger, *The West Somerset Mineral Railway*, 1962

Turner, James, *Ghosts in the South West*, 1973

Underwood, Peter, *Gazetteer of British Ghosts*, 1971; *This Haunted Isle*, 1984

Wood, Sir Evelyn, *British Battles on Land and Sea* (2 volumes), 1915

ALSO AVAILABLE

GHOSTS OF DEVON
by Peter Underwood

GHOSTS OF CORNWALL
by Peter Underwood

WESTCOUNTRY MYSTERIES
Introduced by Colin Wilson

SOMERSET IN THE OLD DAYS
by David Young

UNKNOWN SOMERSET
by Rosemary Clinch & Michael Williams

EXMOOR IN THE OLD DAYS
by Rosemary Anne Lauder

STRANGE SOMERSET STORIES
Introduced by David Foot

AROUND GLORIOUS DEVON
by David Young

RIVERS OF CORNWALL
by Sarah Foot

SUPERSTITION & FOLKLORE
by Michael Williams

OCCULT IN THE WEST
by Michael Williams

ECCENTRICS IN CORNWALL
by June Lander

AROUND BUDE & STRATTON
by Joan Rendell

100 YEARS ON BODMIN MOOR
by E.V. Thompson

SEA STORIES OF CORNWALL
by Ken Duxbury

SEA STORIES OF DEVON
Introduced by E.V. Thompson